PREACH

Sister Preach!

A Collection of Sermons That Uplift and Inspire

Dr. Bettye W. Knighton

*e*merge
Publishing Group, LLC

ISBN 978-0-9818383-1-1

Published by
Emerge Publishing Group, LLC
Riviera Beach, FL
Phone: 888-204-7793
www.emergepublishers.com

DEDICATION

*To my Grandfather,
James Willis "Bud" Freeman,
a brilliant scholar of the Word of God.*

Contents

INTRODUCTION

I clearly remember the days I hid from my grandfather to avoid having to read and expound on a Bible verse. I didn't mind the reading, but struggling to decipher meaning from those verses with words that one can barely pronounce was to be avoided whenever possible. Granddaddy would start reading the Bible right after dinner and continue until he retired for the evening.

I wondered how anyone could read the same book day after day, year after year with unwavering zeal. What held his interest? Why did he love that book so? There was nothing he liked better than a scholarly discussion of some passage of the Bible.

He was not a preacher, but he throughly enjoyed a good sermon. He would come home after church and share pertinent points from the minister's message. Sometimes, he would say to me, "Bett, read this verse and tell me what it means." Reading the verse was no problem, but the other half of that request created problems for me. He would take the same verse that gave me a problem and pick it to pieces. How could so much come from one verse. Unknowingly, that was my first exposure to hermeneutics.

Later, when I attended Roosevelt Junior College, I had a communications instructor who taught us the art of interpretation. That class increased my appreciation for my grandfather who did not have the benefit of formal education. He was blessed by God with extraordinary skills.

I had no idea at the time that he was planting a seed - a seed that did not germinate until twenty-five years later. By then, James Willis Freeman had gone home to be with the Lord. If I could talk to him now, I would tell him that the Word of God is now a part of my daily life. I would tell him that I have shared messages over the last twenty years up and down the Florida East Coast in over twenty churches from Miami to Cocoa Beach. I would tell him that I could really benefit from his expertise in constructing homiletically and hermeneutially sound messages.

I would tell him that while I was in denial, other cousins picked up the mantle and ran with it. Granddaddy, your efforts were not wasted.

I have always loved books and public speaking. Now, add to that a love of the Word and sharing the Word becomes a natural progression. I am not unaware of the sentiment regarding women preachers. I prefer to be called a teacher of the Word rather than a preacher of the Word. But whatever I am called, I know I am a child of God with equal rights to share His Word with anyone willing to listen.

Most of the messages in this collection date back to a period long before I studied Buttrick, Mitchell, Proctor and other great homileticians. I do not claim to have mastered even a fraction of what they taught, but I do claim a strong love for the Word of God and a desire to share it with others.

I pray that the messages offered here will be inspiring and uplifting.

WHEN 'JUST ENOUGH' IS MORE THAN ENOUGH

And she said, as the Lord thy God liveth, I have not a cake, but an handful of meal in a barrel, and a little oil in a cruise: and, behold, I am gathering two sticks, that I may go in and dress it for me and my son, that we may eat it, and die.

I Kings 17:12

The books of Kings record a period in Israel's history that is both triumphant and tragic. It is the historical period that follows the time of the kings from David to Nebuchadnezzar. A few kings were good, but most were bad. Every King that followed David was measured by the standard set by David, but it was a human standard and many failed to reach it. We see the decline and fall of the kingdom. We see that man's rule over God's kingdom had devastating results. The books of Kings teach us that man is unable to rule himself and the world.

Evil Kings dotted the landscape year after year. It's at times when things are at their worse that God sends his best. He sent one of His greatest prophets. He sent Elijah, who came in with a tempest and went out with a whirlwind. God had to have him present at the time that King Ahab ruled the kingdom. Ahab was a spineless, hen-pecked, poor excuse for a man who was married to one of the most evil women that ever walked through the pages of Scripture - Jezebel. She was a vicious vixen, with ice-water in her veins.

One day Elijah, without thinking of danger to himself, strode into the king's court, stood before him and prophesied, saying: "There will be no rain nor dew for years except on my word." He strode out. You know Ahab didn't like that, but he wasn't the one to fear, it was Jezebel.

God told Elijah to go and hide. Things have to be mighty bad for an all powerful God to tell you: "Go hide." Elijah knew he had to go fast and in a hurry, because if Ahab didn't get him, Jezebel would.

Elijah had this habit of speaking out. Prophets were like that. They would speak out no matter the peril to themselves. He was trained to do that, trained by the best - God himself. God had a habit of sending people into barren land and untamed territories to train them. They learned to depend totally on God. He trained Moses in the Desert. He took Abraham out of Ur of the Chaldees and sent him into rugged terrain. He sent John the Baptist into the wilderness. Even Paul spent two years in the Arabian desert when he wasn't in jail. That's the way God trains his men. He has to have their undivided attention.

God didn't just tell Elijah to hide without telling him where to hide. He made sure he was far enough away that he would be safe from the hands of Ahab and Jezebel. There was a brook to supply his water and ravens to feed him. Everyday, they fed him just enough to sustain him. I don't know how long he stayed, but it must have been more than 2 years.

After some time, something started happening; the water supply started drying up. As the weeks and months went by he watched the water get lower and lower. Elijah looked at the drying-up brook and learned a spiritual lesson. He saw that his life was just a dried-up brook. He realized that he was just a channel through which the living water of God could flow. And church, we are dried-up brooks unless the Word of God is flowing through us.

It's time for God to move Elijah again. God sends him to Zarephath where a widow woman has been commanded to sustain him.

Elijah and the widow were two people linked together in God's providential plan. The widow is blessed with the

honor and distinction of sustaining the prophet of God for a little over two years. Why did God pick the widow woman for this honor? I'm sure there were people of means there who were in a much better position to feed the prophet. She was a poor widow who had *just enough* to eke out a living for her and son. Just a single mother like so many single mothers today trying to survive with *just enough*.

What about Elijah? What is his distinction? Who is the man? He's a man that "stands before Jehovah." He's a man who at his words, the clouds are sealed and no rain comes. At his word the heavens open up and the rain falls. He's the same man whose prayer will later bring down fire upon the sacrifice on Carmel. He was the man who was to ride alive into heaven in a chariot of fire. He was the man who many centuries later was destined to appear in glory with Messiah on the mount of transfiguration. Elijah was a man.

God told him about the command to the widow woman. This command was for the good of both of them. Elijah needed food; the widow needed food. When Elijah first saw a widow, he didn't know if she was the one. The fact that she was gathering sticks was not a good sign. This lady must be poor. That's an understatement. She was destitute.

That morning, she got up and looked in the meal barrel. Her heart was crushed. She knew supplies were getting low - but My God - not this low. She had no means of support. Her husband was dead. She thought " What am I going to do? How am I going to feed my son?" As a mother, the hardest thing in the world to do, is to look into the sad eyes of a hungry child and know that you have no food. There was no "Feed the Children" organization, there was no Division of Families and Children. There were no food stamps. There was no welfare system at all. What do you do? I'll tell you what she did.

She went out to gather sticks. The widow had no idea that while she was gathering sticks, she was also on an errand for God. We don't know when God is using us as a vessel to bless someone else. We don't know why He tells us to do certain things. God uses our purposes to work out his own. Man proposes; God disposes.

Elijah asked her for a drink of water. The gift of water to the thirsty is always regarded as a sacred duty in the East. The widow could handle the request for water, but he then asked for a piece of bread. Now, that changed the picture. This was a test. Wait a minute, she can give him water, but bread? She had *just enough* meal to make one small cake of bread, probably what my dad called a ho-cake. He would say, "Sweet, make me one of them ho-cakes." The widow was down to a little oil and a little meal - *just enough* for her and her son.

This widow woman did not understand the divine providence of God. She was ok as long as the prophet only asked for water, but when he asked for bread, she quickly swallowed whatever pride she had left and told Elijah: " I'm gathering these sticks for a reason. I'm going to take my *last* oil and my *last* meal and prepare my *last* supper for me and my son. And then, we're going to lay down, take our *last* breath and die."

Elijah said, " Don't worry about it. You go prepare the meal, but feed me first and if you do that, God says neither your meal nor your oil will run out until He sends the rain again." She could have said, "I don't believe you." She could have said, " Man, you must be crazy, this is just enough for me and my son." But she didn't do that. Her obedience saved her life. Maybe that's why the Word says: *Obedience is better than a sacrifice.* Had that been some of us, we would have had some choice words for Elijah, words that I cannot repeat here. "Give you some of my last meal? Puleeze, you must be out of your mind." Come on, be honest - don't pretend you wouldn't say something along those lines.

Thank God the widow was obedient. The meal didn't waste nor did the oil. For two and a half years they ate everyday. This miracle was similar to the feeding of the five thousand. Jesus took a little boy's lunch and fed a multitude. We also learn that man should not live by bread alone but by the word of God. The Word says, *Never have I seen the righteous forsaken or his seed begging bread.*

I can recall many, many years ago, being in dire straits for a little while. Thank God it was only a little while. My youngest child was a couple weeks old, so I wasn't working. My husband at the time, now deceased, was out of work. It was winter; we had no money, no electricity, no heat. I couldn't cool the baby's milk, couldn't cook what little food was there. I didn't want my parents to know, so I didn't tell them. I was too embarrassed and too proud. Pride will kill you.

But in those little apartments, 1564 West 34th Street #3 behind Miss Pat's store, I had a brook on one side and a raven on the other, neighbors on each side. One worked and one was a housewife. The neighbor on one side brought breakfast and instructed the neighbor on the other side to bring lunch. When she got off work she brought dinner.

But that didn't last long, because somebody in an apartment across the way got wind of that and went and told my daddy. When I looked up Percy Walker was at the door and ordered me to "pack those babies up- you're going home until your husband get some lights on over here." So I understand this widow woman whose situation was worse than anything any of us in here have faced. She faced death by starvation.

We don't face death because there are too many people to help. There are all kinds of ways we can get help today. Many families have stopped here at Pleasant Heights Baptist Church and we have provided funds for food, rent and other emergencies. There is an invisible sign across this church; we can't see it, but people who pass here with a need whether real or perceived can see it. It says: "**Stop here if you need something; this church will help.**"

And they stop, and they get help and sometimes, they even join the church for a little while and they move on, looking for another sign that says "stop here." That's OK. That's why this church is so blessed. We try to do what God has told us to do. If they scam us, that's on them. We do our part.

As I close I say: **What a mighty God we serve**. He supplies our every need. He may not always give us the luxuries, but He will always "*give us this day our daily bread.*" It will be just enough to sustain us for the day. When tomorrow becomes today, He again will "*give us this day our daily bread.*" There are times when just enough is more than enough. The blessings keep coming and coming and somehow our needs are met. Somehow, we make it - in spite of our enemies trying to cut us down. We make it in spite of bumps in the road and unnecessary detours; we make it in spite of disappointments and devious acts of the devil. **WE MAKE IT!** God will take our *"just enough"* and turn it into *more than enough*.

Like Elijah, we have food that the rest of the world doesn't know about. We have food that feeds us physically, but we have a special food that feeds us spiritually. It's done on a daily basis. Remember, when God fed Moses and the Israelites in the wilderness, He told them to gather *just enough* for the day. Don't try to get extra for tomorrow because that will spoil. Get just enough for today, because every day I will supply your needs. They couldn't hoard food. When they gathered more than enough for the day, it would spoil. On the day before the Sabbath, they received enough manna for that day and the Sabbath.

God taught us to trust Him. In the Lord's Prayer, we pray, *Give us this day our daily bread.* The bread for our soul is a daily bread. It's *just enough* for today. If He gave us enough to last forever, we just might forget to pray. He designed it so that we would have to come to Him consistently for our needs. Everyday, He will supply our needs according to His riches in glory. Supplies of grace are granted day by day. We get forgiveness and strength to get us through the day.

We are living off the prayers of today - not tomorrow's prayers.

There are times when just enough is more than enough. This has been proven on earth, but its highest fulfillment will be seen in heaven where the Lamb, who was slain on Calvary, is now in the midst of the throne. This precious Lamb who gave His life for us shall feed us and we will have more than enough.

May God bless and keep you.

DON'T WASH YOUR NETS TOO SOON

Now when he had left speaking, he said unto Simon, launch out into the deep, and let down your nets for a draught. And Simon answering said unto him, Master, we have toiled all the night, and have taken nothing: nevertheless at thy word I will let down the net.

Luke 5:4,5

Jesus was the best preacher that ever lived. Wherever He went He drew large crowds. The people loved good, down to earth preaching. They wanted to hear the Word of God from Jesus because He was a teaching-preacher. There was always a lesson to be learned. No one before, nor anyone since could preach like He did. With Jesus, everyone was able to understand. It wasn't like listening to the Scribes or Pharisees. You ever heard someone who sounded real good but you didn't have a clue to what they were talking about? It wasn't like that with Jesus.

Jesus never had a radio broadcast or a TV ministry that beamed the message to millions. He didn't have a business card and He never had a microphone in His hand. But there was so much power in Him that when He preached, He would turn that place upside down. The place would never be the same again. What started as a few curiosity seekers turned into massive crowds.

So on this day as He stood by the Lake of Genasaret, the crowd pressed upon Him. If they got right up on Him, the masses wouldn't be ever to see Him. Jesus needed to get where the crowds could see Him. He saw two fishing boats standing by the lake with no one on them. The fishermen were outside the boats washing their nets. When the work day was over, it was the custom to wash the nets in preparation for the next day. The fact that the fisherman were washing the nets sent a message that said: " I'm finished. I quit. I resign. I give up. I am convinced that things are not going to get any better."

It means our expectations have been destroyed; our faith has fizzled. It means a spirit of failure has set in. Sometimes we give up too soon. We've given up on our finances. We've given up on our children. We've given up on our careers. So we are not in a position to criticize these men who are washing their nets.

There is actually a spirit of fear that exists. There is definitely a fear of failure. Some people won't start a project if they think they are going to fail. Fear of failure can stop us dead in our tracks. That happens to us sometimes. We just get tired. That happened to Simon and the fisherman. They didn't want to fish another hour because they had fished all night and didn't catch anything. So they washed their nets.

Fear of failure is a serious problem. Some psychologists did a study of this paralyzing emotion. In a huge water tank that housed a shark at a water park, they enclosed the shark in a clear glass cylinder. The food for the shark was placed between the outer wall of the tank and the glass cylinder.

When the shark tried to get his food, he ran into the cylinder which was invisible to him. He backed off and tried another direction with the same results. After several tries, the shark gave up. When the glass cylinder was removed, the food was accessible, but the shark made no effort to reach it because he feared failure once again.

At first glance, this passage of Scripture is easy to look over and not get the main lesson from it. It seems like a normal procedure. But upon looking again, something was amiss. There were no fish in the boat. They had caught nothing, And it was morning. This was their livelihood.

Since the boats weren't being used, Jesus went into the boat that belonged to Simon Peter. He told Simon to push the boat out into the water. Pushing out would make Jesus harder to be heard, but it was better that He be seen. Christ had a strong voice. He preached to thousands at one time with no sound system. We preach to fifty and we demand a microphone.

Jesus came down to the sea to do kingdom business. He came to dispense the infallible, indestructible, awesome Word of God. Every time He preached, he packed the house. His preaching could stop a storm or calm a hurricane. He could wake up out of a dead sleep and preach a three-word sermon: *"Peace Be Still."* Even the forces of nature obeyed him. There was power in every word. He didn't just preach a sermon, He was a sermon. He was Jesus, the mountain mover; Jesus the sickness healer; Jesus the death spoiler.

When He finished teaching the people, Jesus had a lesson for Simon and the fishermen. This was not a Sabbath day; this was a work day, so soon as he finished preaching, he set them to work. This tells us that it is our duty to manage our religious exercises so they may complement our worldly business and to manage our worldly business so that it is not an enemy to our religious exercises. We can't spend all our time and wealth on worldly business and no time with Jesus. Likewise, Jesus does not expect us to neglect our children, family or business. We must have balance.

Jesus told Simon to take the boat out into deep water and let the nets down for a load of fish. The fisherman were not accustomed to fishing in deep waters. They worked at night, when the schools of fish worked in toward shore to feed on the swarms of minnows in the shallower, warmer waters.

Jesus had a two-fold purpose:
    1. Jesus was looking for a place to preach to the

pressing crowd.

2. Jesus is recruiting potential disciples.

It appears here that Jesus is talking to some quitters, losers, deadbeats who gave up with an overnight problem. Some may wonder, why pick these guys, especially if you're only going to pick twelve. Couldn't He make a better choice than this?

While we may look at these men as losers, Jesus sees something else in them. He sees things in people we can't see. And who are we to judge anyway? Some of us may be washing our nets, yet He sees potential in each of us. Jesus has issued a command. He told them to "launch out into the deep." They were hanging out in shallow water. Big fish don't swim in shallow water.

Peter didn't want to accept this command at first. Simon said to Jesus, "Master, we have worked all night and didn't catch a single fish." He was just like some of us. Sometimes we get insulted when we think that people think we didn't try.

Sometimes, we say: " Lord, I know you think I haven't tried, but I've done all I know how to do. I changed all I knew how to change. I worked everything I knew how to work. I toiled all night - a long night, a cold night. I've put forth all this effort, Lord, and I don't have anything to show for it. Lord, I've tried to get out of debt. I'm beginning to think things will never get any better. Master, Master, I'm in situations that I don't like. I don't like poverty. Or arguments or job failure. I don't like bounced checks or failed marriages. Master, I've tried.

Master, By now I should be married. By now I should be on my feet. By now I should be sitting pretty. By now I should be retired. Master, Master, where did I go wrong? I tried, I tried, I know I tried."

When we hit that low point, Jesus Christ is there to listen when we come to Him with our problems. We are not in this alone. Peter assisted Christ in his preaching by providing his boat as a pulpit. Christ accompanied him in his fishing. Peter stayed with Christ at the shore. Christ stayed with him in the deep.

Although Peter and his crew had caught nothing all night long, they were obedient when Christ told them to drop their nets. We'll hang out with Christ in shallow water. But staying with Him in deep waters requires faith and commitment.

The lesson is that after they talked about their failures, they said *nevertheless*. That one word, *nevertheless* provided a miracle. They said, "If you say so Lord, in spite of our past failure, we'll be obedient and drop the net again." In spite of what we go thru, there is a *nevertheless* miracle waiting for us. Don't give up now. It's too soon to wash the nets.

Notice something here in verse 4. Jesus didn't say let down your net. What did He say? He said *nets* - plural.

When Jesus blesses, we need to be prepared to receive a big blessing. But when Peter responded, he said we'll let down our net - singular. Simon had been so disappointed that he really didn't expect much. He let down a net instead of nets.

So when they let the net down, they caught so many fish, the net broke. They received more than they ever dreamed, more than they were prepared to receive. This was one of those '*pressed down, shaken together, running over*" blessings.

They called their partners for help and filled up both boats so full they started to sink. Can you imagine receiving a blessing so great, you have to call your family, friends, enemies, everybody to help you receive it? That's the kind of blessing I'm waiting on. Peter and the others were so amazed that they had caught so much fish in so short a time after working all night and catching none. This tells us that it is not over when we think its over. Sometimes we wash our nets too soon. The blessing might be one step forward or one prayer away.

By this huge catch of fish, Christ showed his dominion over the sea as well as in the dry land, over its wealth as well as over its waves. He re-payed Peter for the loan of his boat. We can never do more for God than He does for us.

As believers in Jesus Christ, we are called into service by the King. We must do our duty and leave the rest to God. When we are tired with our worldly business, we are welcome to come to Christ, and spread our case before Him. We do get tired; that's why Christ told us to "**Come unto me, all ye that labor and are heavy laden and I will give you rest.**"

All we have to do is recognize that we are not very good fisherman - We have to recognize our faults and failures. When we are willing to depend on Him, He will not put us out of the fishing business, and He will not throw us overboard. He will use us. He uses whom He chooses, when He chooses, where He chooses, how He chooses because He is sovereign God.

Peter may have been a failure as a fisherman. But when he went into service with the master, he became a successful fisherman of men. On the day of Pentecost, Peter caught 3,000 men in the gospel net.

We are all disciples of Christ. He had twelve original disciples. One was a curser, one was a doubter, one was a betrayer. The Bible didn't waste time telling of the sins of the other nine. But these twelve men were rejects who turned the world upside down. The world wasn't turned upside down by mega-churches, or industry, but by Jesus and twelve ordinary men.

God is amazing. He can take a messed up painting and turn it into a beautiful masterpiece. That's what He does with us. It's called redemption. It's called restoration. It's what God does best.

Be forewarned. As a believer, you are on the devil's hit list. The enemy is after your mind, he's after your joy, he's after your peace, he's after your self-esteem. He

wants you to quit. He wants you to wash your nets. The enemy will use anything against you. He will use your childhood, your past or your broken home. He will use your broken promises, your broken dreams or your first born.
Satan will kill anything he can to destroy you and keep you from reaching your potential. Whatever you do, don't

quit. Don't wash your nets too soon. Failure is not an option. Life is like riding a bicycle. If you fall, get up and try again until you learn how to ride it. You don't give up.

As I close. I say to you: God will get the glory out of our struggle. This Christian life is a constant fight. It's a fight against poverty, hatred, strife, envy, racism and sexism. But remember, the fight is fixed. In the prize fighting world when a fight is fixed, the insiders - managers and promoters don't get upset if a Boxer A appears to be losing because they know that in the third round B is going is going down and all of their money is on Boxer A.

Well, Christ doesn't get excited if life has us on the ropes, because the fight is fixed. It was fixed in eternity before he sent us forward. It was fixed on Calvary when he stretched wide his hands and hung low his head. It was fixed on resurrection day when He rose with all power in His hands. He knows that in the end, we will win and all of the heaven's resources are on us. Jesus is our manager, our promoter, and our trainer. To God be the glory!

Remember, *We are more than conquerors through Christ Jesus*. Don't quit. Don't give up. Don't give out. Don't give in. Don't wash your nets too soon.

SURVIVING THE STORMS OF LIFE

But the ship was now in the midst of the sea,
tossed with waves; for the wind was contrary.
Matthew 12:24

There are all kinds of storms. Palm Beach County, as well as the entire state of Florida, can attest to the fact that when the storms come, they come fast and furiously with no respect for persons or property. There are personal storms, and storms of nature. In this passage of Scripture, the Disciples were experiencing a storm.

After feeding 5,000 people not including women and children, Jesus instructed his disciples to get into the ship and go to the other side. He would meet them there later. He went up into the mountain to talk with His Father. And sometimes we have to do that. We have to steal away from the crowd, away from all the distractions. We have to go to our secret place and have a talk with our Father.

This story happens on a clear night. The stars were in the sky; you could see the moon. It was a sailor's dream, a perfect night, no sign of trouble anywhere. It's like that sometimes. Everything seems to be going well. It's wonderful. But as they set out in the boat, something happened. The weather changed; the night turned ugly. The stars disappeared. The waves rose to twelve to fifteen feet. The wind started howling like Hurricane Frances and roaring like Hurricane Jeanne. The disciples were reeling and rocking and rowing as hard as they could. I imagine they were terrified.

There is something scary about a storm. I remember sounds those hurricanes made. It seemed that any minute the door was going to blow open. Or the roof was going to lift off. The sound was terrifying. So, I can relate to the fear of the Disciples, after all, they had no cover.

Yet while they were rowing, the unseen God was in the mountains praying. Thank God for somebody praying. I am sure all of us in these storms had relatives or friends somewhere outside of the area praying for us. We were praying, but they were praying, too.

Christ sent the disciples away. Since He is an all-knowing God, didn't He know that He was sending them into a storm? Yes, He did. He didn't do it to frighten them, rather that His power, grace and mercy would be manifested. He trained them step by step to be strong. He knew that one day He would have to leave them and they were going to have to be able to survive the storms of life.

Sometimes, when we start out in life, there is not a cloud in the sky; the water is still. But no sooner we do what God says do or we go where God says go, things become chaotic. Winds everywhere. Storms everywhere. Things falling apart all over the place. And we wonder, "Where are you, God"? We don't see Him, but He's there.

During the fourth watch, the time from 3:00AM to daylight, Jesus walked towards them. They had been rowing for nine hours and had only gone four miles. That's like people who decided at the last minute to evacuate the South Florida area and head north. They found themselves on a highway that resembled a parking lot, barely moving. The Disciples started at 6:00 P.M. and rowed to midnight and they rowed from midnight to 3:00 A.M. And while they were rowing they were reeling and rocking and struggling to keep the boat afloat. But Jesus appeared in the fourth watch.

Today, the church may very well be in the fourth watch. The critical problems of the church serve as an opportunity for Christ to visit and appear for them. Our problems are Christ's opportunities. It's His chance to show us Who He is and what He can do. When we are in trouble, He comes. Maybe not during the first watch, maybe not during the second watch; sometimes it's the last watch of the day, but He comes. I don't know why He waits until the last minute to come to our rescue; Why does He wait until the waves are dashing? Why does He wait until the bills are due and the bank account is on "E"? Why does He wait until I'm at the end of my rope? Well, maybe that's the only time he can command my undivided attention.

When the disciples saw Jesus walking on the water, they were scared; they thought they were seeing a ghost. They thought he was a figment of their imagination. They screamed, "It's a ghost!" They didn't recognize their Master.

That's the problem with us sometimes. We don't recognize Jesus when He comes. We are looking for Him to come at a certain time, in a certain way, and in a certain place. We can't box God in. We can't expect Him to fit our expectations. He operates outside of the box; He's sovereign. He can move anyway He wants to move, come anyway He wants to come, at anytime. And He came.

So many times He has come to us and we missed Him. So many times we have said, "God, show yourself" and the sun comes up in the morning, and we missed him. "God, reveal yourself" and we woke up feeling great - no aches and pains - and we missed Him. "God, show yourself" and someone puts a loving arm around us just when we needed encouragement, but we missed Him. So many times He has flung a rainbow in the sky after a rainy day, and we missed Him. We are still alive after surviving multiple hurricanes. Did we miss Him? All we have to do is look around us and we can see the evidence of God all over the place.

Fear can blind us and keep us from seeing the Savior. That's what happened here. Jesus knew that the disciples were terrified. He quickly said to them, "It is I, Don't be afraid."

Peter said, "Lord, if it's you, bid me come to you."

Notice in our text that Peter did not say "if it is you, I'll come to you." He said, "bid me come to you", in other words *let* me come to you. We need to wait on our call. Wait before we step into troubled waters. But when Christ says, "come", it's time to get out of the boat. There should be no hesitation or procrastination.

When He says, "Come", It's time to step out of our comfort zones. We get too comfortable in our positions, our places, and sometimes, we don't want to move. But in order to go to another level in Christ, we may have to experience a storm.

And so Peter stepped out walked on the water. The winds started howling like a category 4 hurricane and Peter momentarily took his eyes off the Savior. When he was walking and looking at Christ Jesus, he was all right. But when he took his eyes off Jesus, that's when he started sinking.

It was fear that caused a problem for Peter. Fear creeps up on us; it is mixed with courage and faith. Peter had the *courage* to get out of the boat, the *faith* that Christ could keep him, but there was a little fear mixed in. That fear caused him to take his eyes off Christ. We start out on our journey as Peter did with faith. But if our troubles last too long, our faith begins to waver.

Peter had the good sense to cry out, **"Lord, Save me."** He didn't have time for a long prayer. Peter prayed an "*arrow*" prayer. It didn't go left or right, it went straight to the source. "Lord, save me." And no sooner was it said than the Lord reached out His hand and caught him and said, "O, you of little faith, why did you doubt me?"

And that's a good question. He walked with Christ, was taught by Christ. He watched him heal the sick, give sight to the blind, raise the dead and feed the hungry. Why did he doubt him?

When the Savior took Peter and got in the boat, the storm died immediately. That amazed the disciples. Out of all the miracles Jesus performed, this amazed them. They had been in trouble before in the boat but Jesus was with them asleep. They woke him up and said, "Master don't you care if we perish." Jesus spoke and said "Peace, be still" And the storm died. This time he didn't say anything, He just stepped into the boat and the storm disappeared as quickly as it had come.

And they said, "Surely, you are the Son of God." They worshiped Him. God shouldn't have to perform a miracle every other day for us to recognize Him as the Savior.

We can learn a lesson from this passage of scripture. Whenever we decide to follow Jesus, we can expect our storms to be more frequent and more violent.

When it's storming, boat owners tie up their boats by the docks and put protective covering on the side to keep the boats from being damaged as they bounce back and forth against the docks. But an old sailor said, in a storm, don't tie the boat up at the dock, take the boat out in the open sea, and drop the anchor deep. The boat is made to handle the storm and the anchor keeps it from floating away. The winds may blow and the waves may dash and that boat will rock from side to side, but it won't sink.

That's what we have to do - We've got to anchor deep in Christ so that when the storms do come, and they will come if we are serving Christ, we won't sink under the burden of our storm.

The wind will blow us from side to side, but if we're anchored deep in Christ, we will survive the storm. Anchor deep and ride the storm.

There is a song that says: *In times like these, you need an anchor, In times like these you need a savior. Be sure - very sure that your anchor holds and grips the solid rock.* That rock is Jesus.

Hɪᴅᴅᴇɴ Tʀᴇᴀsᴜʀᴇ

And when the Lord saw that Leah was hated,
He opened her womb, but Rachel was barren.

Genesis 29:31

This passage of scripture is very familiar. We know the story. Jacob in collaboration with his mother, Rebecca, deceived his Father, Isaac, and tricked his brother out of his birth right. He had to leave home. His mother sent him to her brother, Laban. There he saw the beautiful daughter of Laban, Rachel. He fell madly in love with her.

He promised to work seven years for Rachel. On the wedding night, his bride was heavily veiled as was the custom. In the morning, as daylight peeped through the tent, he realized instead of his beloved Rachel, it was Leah.

Laban perpetrated fraud on Jacob. The fraud was deliberate, bold and selfish. But it was a kind of a "payback." There are sins in this world which are often punished in kind. Jacob, the "trickster" got tricked. The chickens had come home to roost. Jacob had deceived his Father and now he had been deceived. Leah was an unfortunate pawn in a cruel game between Laban and Jacob. You could even say she was a booby prize.

The scripture says that Leah was tender-eyed; but Rachel was beautiful and well-favored. Leah is one of the few women in the scriptures of whom it's said that she was not particularly beautiful. Saying she was "tender-eyed" is a nice way of saying she was ugly. She could not begin to compare with her sister Rachel.

The world has always had its standard of beauty. And it was no different during biblical days. Leah didn't meet those standards. She must have asked herself a hundred times, "Why couldn't I be beautiful like my sister?" Leah didn't realize it, but this is a dangerous question to ask God. Why? Because God made us like He wanted us to be. Some have brown eyes, Some have blue eyes. Some have long hair, some have short hair. Some are tall, some are short. It's a slap in God's face to look at someone else and say, I wish I were more like her. God uniquely designed us just the way He wanted us to be. He made us for His glory.

When we compare ourselves to other people, it's like

saying, "God, you made a mistake. You failed. Why did you have to make my nose so big? Why did you have to make my lips so thin? Why couldn't you make me tall? You could have done a better job creating me." This is a big mistake. We do not have the right to question or criticize God.

He is our creator and after creation, God said, "It is good." When He created the world, He said "It is good." When He created man, He said, "It is good." When He created Leah, He said "It is good." When He created you and me, He said "It is good." So who are we to look down on other people or ourselves because we or they don't meet some arbitrary standard of beauty.

The problem in this situation arises as a result of the difference in the way these two women were treated. One was treated like a queen, like something precious, something special. The other one - she was just there. She probably didn't even get a decent good morning. She was just there - In the way of Rachael and Jacob.

Think about this. How must it feel to have a husband....He was yours first. Now another lady comes into the picture and is sharing him and she gets all of the attention. How must Leah have felt? She's nothing special to look at. She already knows it. And every time she looks at her beautiful sister, every time she sees the way Jacob looks at Rachel, she hurts. How painful must that be? What is she to do? She went day by day wondering, why did this happen to me? Why was I born like this, Why couldn't I be pretty? Question, questions and no answers.

Then one day, God, the Father, looked down. He said my

child is being mistreated. That's my creation. It's time for me to get involved. Our God will only allow us to suffer so much pain. When it starts getting to be unbearable, he'll step in every time. Won't He do it? Rachel's treasure was her beauty. Everyone could see it. But no one could see Leah's treasure because it was locked up on the inside. When God saw how she was despised, he unlocked that hidden treasure. He opened up her womb and she started to bear children. That was her treasure. God does everything in His own time.

When God says its time for your ministry to blossom, neither the devil in hell nor any of his demons can stop you. When it's time for your church to grow, man can't stop it. When God says its time - you can start that new business with confidence. When God says its time, you can step forth boldly and do what thus says the Lord. God will let you know when its time.

Leah's time had come. When her first son Reuben was born, Leah praised God because He had looked favorably upon her. She thought her husband would love her. Nothing changed in the relationship. Rachel was still the favored one. But God wasn't through yet. Leah had more treasure to be revealed. She had more blessings coming. You see when God starts blessing us, He just keeps on blessing.

Leah's treasure was no longer hidden. God gave her Simeon and comforted her. In God's eyes, Leah was not a victim. God kept right on blessing Leah. When Levi was born, she rejoiced because now she thought: "My husband will love me." All Leah wanted was to be loved. That's all she wanted. She wasn't asking for the sun and moon, all she wanted was love. Isn't that what we all want - to be loved? Mankind may not love us but God has a love for you and me that can not be equaled.

Leah still had treasure that was hidden in her womb. When she gave birth to her fourth son, Judah, she said, "Now I will praise the Lord." Leah didn't know just how prominent her place would be in history. Leah's sister had two sons - Joseph and Benjamin - but the glory of the Lord is not expressed in the children of Rachel. The lord's praise is in Judah only, for Judah means "He who praises God."

Both sisters had children. What is significant about Leah's treasure? Why was her treasure different? Because one of those boys, the fourth son, was Judah. Jesus, the Messiah, came through that line from this ugly little woman whom everybody overlooked. People can walk right by you and not see you, not speak to you. You have no worth to them. To them, you have no value. They just don't know what God has inside of you. They don't know about that hidden treasure. And what He has for you, it is for you and nobody can take it away.

So, I came to tell you today, don't deal in the superficial; deal in things of the Spirit. Looks, like flowers and grass, wither and fade away.

It is evident that God had a hand in all that happened to these two sisters. In His independent sovereignty, God created Rachel beautiful and Leah ugly. Out of the beautiful and ugly of those sisters, a tragedy evolved. But something good happened, too. God's choice is not based on outside appearances.

It was not the beautiful Rachel, but the unattractive Leah who was His selection. It was not Rachel, but Leah who was to bear Judah, and therefore become an ancestor of the Christ. God's praise springs forth from Leah, not Rachel.

This follows the rule that what repels human eyes attracts the eyes of God. Man might see ugly, God sees beauty. God does not see things the way we see them. And I'm glad about it. There are two kinds of beauty, ladies. There is a beauty which God gives at birth and which withers as a flower. We can make Mary Kay and Fashion Fair rich, but at some point the wrinkles will come, the hair will gray and no matter how many face lifts are done, age will show eventually. But there's another kind of beauty which God grants when by His grace we are born again. That kind of beauty never vanishes but blooms forever.

Church, there's an important lesson in this passage. We need to learn a lesson from Leah. She spent too much time wanting to be someone else.

We have to know who we are in Christ. Not who man says we are, not who the magazines say we are or the TV ads showing someone in a size 2 dress. We can't all be size 2's; we weren't meant to be the same color, size or shape. We have to know who we are and we have to know that we are divinely, uniquely created by the Master. When He made this flower garden, He made some of us roses, some of us carnations, some begonias. There are even some periwinkles among us. But all of us make up the beauty of God's flower garden.

As creations of God, we are destined for greatness. But

the sad thing is that sometimes we live and die without tapping into that greatness, without seeking to find where our greatness lies. Rachel's greatness was in her outward beauty, Leah's greatness was in her womb.

We as women need to get to the place where we hold a high opinion of ourselves based on the fact that God made us exactly, precisely, intricately, wondrously, and uniquely the way we are. And we have a responsibility to teach this to our daughters. They have the wrong role models. They look at too much BET. They have false impressions of beauty. We need to teach them that it's not about how much flesh you can show or how tight your skirts are or how deep your split is. We need to teach them what real beauty is all about. Titus tells us that the older women must teach the younger women. Have you ever watched young ladies as they walk to school or to the bus stop? Do you wonder if there was a responsible adult at home when they left? They appear to be dressed more for a night club than school. And don't mention the young men with the multicolored, technicolor underwear.

What Leah needed to know, and we need to remember, is that outward beauty fades with time, but the inner beauty that comes from having Christ within is lasting. God made us for His own purpose so that we might reflect a unique aspect of His glory. When we stop comparing ourselves to others and refuse to be intimidated by what other people think and say, then and only then will we be in a position to release the hidden treasure that God has given all of us. My treasure is not the same as your treasure. Your treasure is different from your sister's treasure.

I feel bad for Leah, not because she didn't have the beauty

of her sister, but because she died without knowing how great she was. Her treasure was not really evident until forty generations later. If only Leah had known and understood that it's not the outer beauty that makes you special, but the beauty that you have deep within.

If only she had known that she was the mother of a mighty nation, mother of six leaders of the twelve tribes of Israel. If only she had known that her fourth son was a kingly line that would produce David. If only she had known that same line would later produce the Savior, the Promised Messiah, Jesus himself. I feel sure if she had known all of this she would have stepped a little lighter, walked a little taller, smiled a little broader, prayed a little longer, sang a little louder, danced a little harder. But she didn't know. God knew what the future held for Leah and He knows what the future holds for us because it's all in His hands.

If I could step out of the present and into the past, I would have a little talk with Leah. I would tell her about one of her descendants, David: the little shepherd boy who grew into a might military leader; who slew Goliath and became the second King of Israel. David, who said: *"I will praise thee, for I am fearfully and wonderfully made. Marvelous are thy works. And that my soul knows right well."* David who said: *"Bless the Lord, O my soul and all that's within me. Bless His holy name."* David who said: *"The earth is the Lord's and the fullness thereof, and all they who dwell therein."* And then to really convince Leah of her permanent place in history, I would tell her about my Savior - Jesus Christ.

When Leah lived, the prophet Isaiah had not yet foretold

of the coming Messiah. I would tell Leah that Jesus was born of a virgin, fathered by the Holy Ghost. I would tell her of His earthly ministry, how He healed the sick, gave sight to the blind, raised the dead. And then I would tell Leah of how He came to save those who were lost, how He said: *"For God so loved the world that He gave His only begotton Son, that whosoever believe in him should not perish, but have everlasting life."*

I would tell Leah that one day, on Golgotha's Hill, He was crucified. The grave could not hold Him down. On the third day, He rose with all power in His hands. We have an advantage on Leah. We know all of this. That's why we should be lifting the roofs off in praise and thanksgiving every time we enter the House of God. Know who you are in Christ and serve Him with ever fibre of your being. God bless you.

ARE YOU DRESSED TO KILL?

Put on the whole armor of God, that you may be able to stand against the wiles of the devil.

Ephesians 6:11

Ladies, would you step outside your door in 20 degree weather without your coat on?

Would you walk outside in a blistering rain without your raincoat?

Well, when we step outside our house in any kind of weather, we not only need to be properly dressed, we need to be dressed to kill.

Why?

Because we are living in a world where madmen fly airplanes into buildings and kill thousands of people.

We are living in a world where young girls and boys are being snatched from their own homes and brutally assaulted and murdered.

We are living in a world where greed has taken over and CEO's and CPO's and CPA's are bleeding companies dry and leaving millions of retirement accounts and futures in ruins.

We are living in a world where right here in Palm Beach County, 4000 homeless people - half of them children- sleep on the streets and under bridges every night..

We are living in a world where the word "GOD" is considered politically incorrect, a world where an attempt was recently made to remove the phrase "under God" from the Pledge of Allegiance.

What kind of world is this, where the Creator, Sustainer, and Governor of the universe is no longer welcome?

What kind of world is this?

It's a world where we need to be armored by God for spiritual warfare. It's a world where we need to be dressed to kill.

If you are wondering if there really is a spiritual battle being waged in the heavenlies, let me ask you a question. Have you ever prayed for something? From the depths of your soul you prayed. You waited for an answer, but the answer didn't come. Did you find yourself questioning God? "God, are you listening, do you hear me, God? Where are you, God? I need an answer." But the answer didn't come.

This happened to the prophet Daniel, the same Daniel who used the lion as a pillow. This same Daniel prayed one day, he didn't get an answer, but he didn't stop praying. He prayed and he prayed and he prayed. On the 21st day an angel stood before Daniel and said, "Daniel, the very day you prayed, God heard you and He dispatched an answer immediately. But the Prince of Persia intercepted the angel with the answer. He outranked him. The angel had to call for Michael, the archangel, the warring angel."

Something was happening in the heavenlies. A battle was raging in the spiritual realm. Daniel had no way of knowing why it was taking so long for his prayer to be answered. It happens to us sometimes. Sometimes an answer is on its way and the enemy gets in the way. But we have to keep praying. I told you that to let you know that spiritual warfare is real. It is not some imagined hocus-pocus; it exists. It was real in Daniel's day and it is real today.

That's why it's so important to study the armor that God has given us. I want to tell you how all of this came about.

In Ephesians, Paul gives the armor we should have: our loins girted about with truth, the breastplate of righteousness, shoes of peace, shield of faith, helmet of salvation, sword of the spirit and that ultimate weapon, prayer.

When Paul was writing this letter to the Ephesians, he was

in a Roman prison. Satan wanted him in jail for one reason and the Lord wanted him in jail for another reason.

Paul was treading into Satan's territory and making a dent into his kingdom. He probably said, "I've got to do something about that boy, Paul. He's getting beside himself. He used to work for me when he was persecuting Christians. Now he's preaching and people are leaving me and going over to the Lord's side. But if he's in prison, he is limited to a small audience." Satan thought he could hold back the gospel.

On the other hand, the Lord wanted Paul in jail because he had a job for Paul to do. Now, Paul was a busy man - planting churches during his missionary journeys. But God needed to have Paul's undivided attention. What better way to get it than to have him in a jail cell. While in jail, Paul had nothing to do and nowhere to go.

The Holy Spirit began to work. Paul studied the Roman soldier that was assigned to guard him. He had on all his weaponry. From his head to his toe, this Roman soldier was dressed to kill.

At that time, the Romans had the best equipped, the best dressed soldiers in all the world. There is nothing better looking than a soldier in uniform. I know. I have an ex-solder - shoes spit shined, pants creased just so, hat at just the right angle. And don't let looks fool you. That soldier is trained to shoot a weapon programmed to hit a target 27 miles away.

Soldiers don't just look good, but they are equipped to do battle with the fiercest enemy. We too, need to do more than just look good, talk good, sound good. We have our "hallelujahs" in place, and all our "praise the Lords" just right and we got our little shout in step. But we've got to do more than that. We've got to have the whole armor of God on. We've got to be dressed to kill. After all, we are in the Lord's army and our Commander in chief is Jesus Christ.

Let me caution you. Don't give too much credit to the devil. We tend to blame him for every thing. When Adam and Eve sinned in the garden, Adam blamed it on Eve and we have been shifting blame every since. Sometimes, we are the blame for what happens to us.

Examples:
1. **The devil is attacking my finances**. Well, what do you expect when you spend the household money on that new Gucci bag or cruise on the gambling ship twice a week? The devil didn't do that; you did.

2. **The devil is attacking my health**. You're only sick because of those extra helpings of chittlin's and that double dose of salt on your food. Of course, two slices of sweet potato pie and a triple scoop of Butter Pecan ice-cream didn't help matters either.

3. **My marriage is under attack**. Don't even go there. You never have a kind word for your husband. He hasn't had a decent home-cooked meal in a couple weeks. You spend more time on the phone talking to your girlfriends than you spend talking with him. The devil doesn't have to attack your marriage. You're doing a pretty good job.

However, there are genuine surprise attacks that catch us

off guard. The enemy does come to steal, kill and destroy.

It's time to get dressed. Paul said, *"stand therefore having your loins girted about with truth."*

The question is why did Paul, with all his brilliance start out talking about the ugliest part of the soldiers uniform. The loinbelt was the ugliest, the least noticeable, the least attractive of the soldiers uniform. He could have started out talking about the helmet. It was something to see - intricate, exquisitely beautiful. Or the breastplate - blindingly brilliant with light. Or the shoes, unmatched by anything Aigner, Ferragamo or Stacey Adams ever produced. Or the shield, a work of art with six layers of tightly woven leather. Or the sword, so sharp, so powerful, that you would be dead before you realize you'd been cut.

Now, just a little question for the ladies right now. If you see a brother dressed to kill and you describe him to your sisters, would you start out saying, "He had on a pretty belt?" Come on now - the brother has on a thousand dollar suit, six-hundred dollar pair of shoes, a two-hundred dollar hat, a three-hundred dollar tie, a hundred-dollar shirt - looking like a million bucks and you start out talking about his belt? That's what Paul did. But, there's a method to his madness. Paul did that because he was following the dictates of the Holy Spirit. The Holy Spirit is not just our comforter, he's our guide, our teacher. And if the Holy Spirit was good enough for Paul to follow, he's good enough for us.

The loinbelt of truth is the written word of God. It is the

most important weapon that we possess. Notice the Holy Spirit's approach with Paul. He didn't tell Paul to start with the helmet or the breastplate. He went straight to the middle of the man and started with his belt. God is making a point. The thing that is in the middle of the man is the most important to the man. If you take that weapon off, the man will fall apart.

There are two kinds of the word of God. There is *logos*, which is the written word, and there is *rhema* which is the fresh and revealed word of God. If we ignore our loin belt - our Bible - and lay it aside, we eventually begin to lose our sense of righteousness. If we lay it aside, we will slowly begin to lose our sense of peace. If we lay it aside, we will feel the joy of our salvation begin to deplete.

Be mindful of the fact that neither praise nor worship is the loinbelt. Social gatherings and church fellowships are not the loinbelt. Prayer is not the loinbelt. Only the loinbelt will hold everything together. There is no substitute for the loinbelt.

"..and having on the breastplate of righteousness..."
When we know that God has made us righteous, when we have on that breastplate of righteousness, fixed firmly in place, it doesn't matter how many arrows the enemy shoots against us, because not one arrow will penetrate. It doesn't matter how much they try to condemn us, not one allegation will come our way if we are walking in the breastplate of righteousness. Scripture does not tell that weapons will not be aimed at us. But it does tell us that no weapon formed against us will prosper. When we are dressed in righteousness, we are dressed in armor, we are dressed in the Lord Jesus Christ.

"..and your feet shod with the preparation of the gospel of peace..." The Holy Spirit used killer shoes to describe peace because peace is an awesome weapon. It is a defensive and offensive weapon. Peace will not only protect you; peace is also a brutal weapon. If you use it right, it will keep your spiritual enemies where they belong - under your feet. One good kick and the enemy is crushed.

"..Above all taking the shield of faith..." This weapon is attached to the Word of God - the loinbelt of truth. Where there is no Word, there is no faith. Where there is no faith, the Word of God is absent. Faith and the word of God are inseparable. That's why Paul said, *"Faith comes by hearing and hearing by the Word of God."*

As Paul studied that Roman soldier, he noticed the soldier's shield was covered with layers of leather that had to be oiled daily, otherwise it would become hard and brittle. Because the shield is representative of our faith, this tells us that our shield of faith requires frequent anointing of the Holy Spirit. Without a fresh touch of the Spirit's power upon our lives, our faith will become hard, stiff and brittle. David understood this. He said, *"I shall be anointed with fresh oil."*

There is an unseen connection between the power of God and the operation of faith in our lives and when these two are working hand in hand they build a wall between us and the enemy that cannot be penetrated.

"..And taking the helmet of salvation...." Why did the soldier need a helmet? Well, because his enemy carried a short-handled ax called a battle-ax. When battle-axes were

used, heads rolled. So this helmet wasn't just beautiful, it was intended to save the solder's head and his life. That's what salvation will do for us when we wear it like a helmet on our head. If we don't walk in our salvation and all that it entails, we may feel the brunt of the enemy's battle-ax coming to attack our mind and steal our victory.

Salvation is the most gorgeous, intricate, elaborate, ornate gift God ever gave us. And it didn't cost us anything, but it cost God everything. Salvation is a precious gift, wrapped in sacrifice and tied with the blood of the Savior.

"..And the sword of the Spirit which is the Word of God..." We already know that the loinbelt of truth is the written Word of God. The sword of the spirit represents the rhema word. This is the spoken word, a specific word which the Holy Spirit quickens in our heart and mind at a specific time for a specific purpose.

Noah received a word from God that saved him and his family from destruction. Abraham received a word to leave Mesopotamia and started his walk of faith. Joseph received a word about his personal life through two dreams. Mary, the Mother of the Lord Jesus Christ, received a word from God that is still working wonders in the world today.

"..Praying with all prayer and supplication...." Paul did not compare this to a weapon. But if we had to compare it, we could use the soldier's lance. That is a weapon like a spear with a poisonous tip on the end. This weapon could be hurled at a foe some distance away. Prayer is a powerful tool. It is thrown forward into the spirit realm against the works of the adversary. By hurling this divine

instrument into the face of the enemy, we have the power to stop major obstacles from developing in our personal lives.

And now, our armor is complete. We are armored by God for spiritual warfare. We are dressed to kill.

Having given all the armor, there's some good news and I close with that good news.

Two-thousand years ago in a place called Calvary on Golgotha's hill stood three crosses. Three men - , but the man in the middle was both human and divine. He was special. He was our Lord and Savior Jesus Christ. And the minute his blood spilled to the ground, the minute the ground opened up to receive his blood, the minute he hung his head and died, that minute - that very minute, Satan was defeated. The cross and the resurrection spelled disaster for Satan.

He knew that he was defeated; he's banking on our not knowing that. We have the armor and we have the victory. We have to stand. We don't have to advance, we just have to stand our ground. What we cannot afford to do is retreat. We cannot turn our backs on the enemy. None of the armor that God gave us protects the back. That means we have to stand to face our enemy. It's time. It's time we stop fighting each other and unite for a common cause. He's taken away our children, he's destroyed families, he has nations in chaos, he's wrecking havoc. That's because we stood back and didn't fight. It's time.

It's time to circle the wagons. It's time to close ranks. But before we can do that, we've got to come together. We have families in disarray - splintered. We have church families in discord, divided. The Christian family is not united. We've got to come together in unity and in love.

We are like these fingers. When we are spread out - separated, anything can come between us and weaken us. But when we close ranks, come together and LOCK, THERE IS NOTHING IN HELL OR EARTH THAT CAN PULL THIS UNION APART. He will go somewhere else and find an easier target.

This is what we have to do today. It's time to love one another. It's time to put the full armor on and stand as one unit. It's time to stand and tell the adversary, no more - no more. We're taking back our children, our families, our cities, our nation.

We have been given the armor and the power to do this. Because the same Christ, this victorious Christ who single-handedly defeated the devil lives in us. That's why the apostle John told us - *"Greater is He who is in us than He who is in the world."*

May God bless and keep you.

LIVING SACRIFICES

I beseech you therefore, brethren, by the mercies of God, that ye present your bodies a living sacrifice, holy, acceptable unto God, which is your reasonable service. And be not conformed to this world: but be ye transformed by the renewing of your mind, that ye may prove what is that food, and acceptable, and perfect, will of God.

Roman 12:1,2

The theme today is: "*Christian Men and Women Living According to the Will of God In A Wicked and Perverse Society.*" Wicked. Perverse. Terrible words. Let me share what Random House Webster's College Dictionary has to say about these two words.

PERVERSE - willfully determined not to do what is expected or desired; turned away from what is right, good or proper; contrary; corrupt; wayward and cantankerous.

WICKED - evil or morally bad, sinful, iniquitous, unjustifiable, dreadful; beastly, spiteful, vicious.

For those of you who view the world through rose-colored glasses, maybe you are not convinced that this is the kind of world we are living in today.

What about the sniper with the high-powered rifle that randomly killed eight people? That's wicked. What about the rampart spread of child pornography over the Internet? That's perverse.

What about the proliferation of Saturday night specials and illegal drugs that are destroying African-American families and communities? That's wicked.

And how about the abduction and murders of children taken from their own homes or snatched in public places? That's perverse.

There are crooked CEO'S and CPA's who have bled corporations and wiped out retirement accounts of people who have worked all of their lives and now, in their golden years, find themselves with nothing. That's wicked.

There are scam artists that prey on the elderly and take advantage of their loneliness, trick them out of their life savings. That's perverse.
There are people so consumed with so much hate that they

take airplanes, turn them into missiles, fly them into buildings and kill thousands of people. And because of this act, we are at war with the blood of Americans and Iraqis being spilled in the sands of Iraq.

What are we to do? What are our options? Paul tells us in Phil 2:15: *"That ye may be blameless and harmless, the sons of God, without rebuke, in the midst of a crooked and perverse nation, among whom ye shine as lights in the world."*

Even in the midst of all the evil, the wickedness, we are to be lights in the world. We must live according to the will of God. But, what is God's will for us?

Listen to what the Word of God says: I Peter 1:16 - *"As it is written, Be ye Holy, for I am holy."* I Thess 4:3a *"For this is the will of God, even your sanctification...."*

Two important words: Holiness and Sanctification. To be holy is to have a spiritually pure quality; it means being dedicated to the service of God. To sanctify means to make pure or holy.

We become holy through sanctification. Sanctification is the gracious work of the Holy Spirit whereby the believer is freed from sin and exalted to holiness of heart. How can we live a sanctified life in this sinful world? Let's take a look at Romans 12:1-2.

"I beseech you therefore, brethren, by the mercies of God, that ye present your bodies a living sacrifice, holy, acceptable unto God, which is your reasonable service."

I beseech you...I beg you. He's not just asking gently...I beg you, brothers *by the mercies of God* - God has plenty of mercy - *to present your bodies*...to yield your bodies, this temple of the Holy Ghost. Yield it. This body represents all that we are, our mind our soul, our will. Yield this body. *Yield a living sacrifice.*

God does not want a dead sacrifice. Dead sacrifices are for the old testament. God wants a living sacrifice. God's will for us?...**HOLINESS.** That's His will for us, church - to be Holy and acceptable. You can't be acceptable unless you are first holy.

The will of God is not some mysterious and irrational form of holiness. It is simple and straightforward - to live a holy life that is good in itself - satisfying and complete.

"I beseech you brethren by the mercies of God that you present your bodies a living sacrifice holy, acceptable unto God, which is your reasonable service."

"And be not conformed to this world: but be ye transformed by the renewing of your mind, that you may prove what is that good and acceptable, and perfect will of God."

Be not conformed to this world - Don't pattern your life and conduct by those around you, even those in the church. Because some people wrap the cloak of Christianity around them at 11:00 on Sunday morning and remove it by 2:00 Sunday afternoon. They are Sunday Christians and they go to church on Sundays to get their halos shined.

If you see them on Monday, you won't recognize them because they have blended in with the rest of the world. They are talking like the world, dressing like the world, living like the world, halos rusty and hangin' off the side of their head. In a poem by Matilda Edwards entitled "The Church Walking With the World", she says: "Then the Sons of the world and the Sons of the Church walked closely hand and hard, and only the Master who knoweth all, could tell the two apart."

How can we draw the lost to Christ if they can't see anything special in us? We need to watch ourselves.

But be ye transformed - Be ye changed... like metamorphous, changing from one form to another. Like from a tadpole to a frog - you become something completely different. Or a caterpillar to a butterfly - you don't even look the same.

We must dare to be different. The transforming of our minds will strengthen our will and we will be able to discern the will of God. One way to transform is to hide His word in our heart.

By permitting the Spirit of God to renew our mind, we will be able to test the will of God and find it good. The minute that you and I assume a pose and pretend to be something we are not, it is impossible for us to determine the will of God for our lives.

By the renewing of our mind - The renewing of the mind is the renewing of the whole man, for out of it are the issues of life.

The acceptable and perfect will of God - The will of God is good, and acceptable and perfect. It is good for us. It is acceptable and pleasing to God. The only way to attain His favor is to conform to His will.

These two verses are the Christian's calling:
1. Consecration - Present your bodies
2. Separation - Be not conformed
3. Transformation - Be ye transformed; changed

The last four words in this verse are key- perfect will of God. Not my will, not your will, but God's will. God's will is that we live holy.

Those of us who do not seek after God, who do not find out what His will is for us, who do not walk in his will, live His will, will be lost. This is not an easy world to live in. It's wicked, perverse and it grows more so every day. Although we are surrounded by all the mess, we still have to live holy.

Living Holy. What does that involve? It involves a complete surrender to God. It involves leading exemplary lives. It involves overcoming desires of the flesh and walking in the Spirit. When we look around us, we see people who are supposedly holy, but they're not setting good examples for our children, our young men and our young ladies. People watch us. And they know if we're real or if we're fake.

They know if this gospel being preached is generic or the real thing. Be careful. Paul tells us in Titus that the old women should teach the young women. If you're in church, you're living holy, you have an obligation to teach someone else. We teach, not to condemn, but to touch lives in a positive manner.

If you look at some of the young girls going to and from school, it's clear that somebody has been falling down on the job. It's hard to believe they are actually going to class. When I see them, I wonder was anybody home when they left? Was there an adult in the house when they left to go to school? Their clothes, four sizes to small, seem to be more appropriate for a night club, belly buttons showing, everything else showing. Somebody has not been teaching these young ladies how to dress properly. You don't have to look like a little old lady to be properly dressed. Who is teaching these young women? Their mothers aren't teaching them because they weren't taught.

Young men are walking down the street, hanging' on the corners, with plaid, striped and polka dot underwear showing. Don't you get tired of seeing their underwear? Ever wonder what would happen if their hands were full and they had to run from trouble?

Who's teaching them? What kind of lessons are they learning? Where is their instruction? Some of these children are from single family homes. They need mentors. **Where are the mentors from the church?** These families need prayers of saints.

There are seventeen years between me and my youngest sister. As the years go by, things get harder, there are more distractions and temptations. Mom wore out a set of knees on the younger bunch; she is now wearing out the second set of knees on grands and great grands.

Being sanctified does not mean a little old lady in a long white dress with nappy hair and no make-up. It means someone living a life that is acceptable to Jesus Christ. The Bible tells us all we need to know about Godly, holy living. Sanctification is the work of the Holy Spirit - the act of God's grace by which "our old man is crucified' and the moral nature is cleansed of all unrighteousness.

This is the will of God, even your sanctification. There are positive results of sanctification and holiness. The very first one is **love**. Paul tells us that the love of God is shed abroad in our heart by the Holy Ghost who is given unto us. God loves us, and we in turn must love others. Another one is Assurance. There is no more guessing - I think I'm a Christian or I think I'm saved. When you have been filled with God's Spirit, you can sing that song: *I Know I've Been Changed, The angels in Heaven done signed my name.* After the Spirit takes up residence in our hearts there is an assured confidence in God's salvation. God said, *"Ye shall be witnesses unto Me."*

We need to be witnesses because In the courts of this wicked and perverse world, Jesus is still on trial. His cause and His gospel are on trial. We can not be good witnesses in the defense of Jesus Christ unless we have a soul experience of some significance. We can't give a testimony about something we know nothing about.

There are many other effects of living holy; peace, sensitiveness and courage. The most important effect is the endowment of the Holy Spirit. This effect - Holy Spirit Power - is the one that most affects the growth of the church.

This is the effect that will cure the disease of the church. Many of our churches are sick and dying a slow death. I'm not talking about numbers, but actual converts. These churches can benefit from Holy Ghost Power.

When Jesus rose from the dead the whole church of Christ could assemble in one upper chamber. At the time Jesus ascended unto the Father, it numbered 120. We know we're living in a wicked and perverse world now. It was just as bad then. It was the age of universal corruption. Outside of Judea, idolatry reigned supreme. Gods and goddesses everywhere, representing every vice you can imagine, even a stature for THE UNKNOWN GOD. These idol gods were openly worshiped in magnificent temples. All of the power was in the hands of a heartless imperialism.

The people were sunk in hopeless degradation, without means, without learning, without protection, and sixty million of them in the Roman Empire alone were slaves.

Elderly parents died of starvation, children were exposed and murdered. Men fought each other to the death in the arena just to provide entertainment to a blood-thirsty crowd. Christians were thrown into the arena and ferocious lions were turned lose as the crowds cheered. Every precept of the moral law was violated almost without conscience.

The early disciples were effective although they had no wealth, no social position, no prestige, no government aid, no help from established institution. There were despised. They had no influence, no skill, and no education. Neither the Old nor the New Testament was in the hands of the people. They had no Christian literature nor a single Christian house of worship. Pomp, power, custom and public sentiment were all against them. They were reproached, reviled, persecuted, and subjected to exile and death. They all died martyrs for the sake of the gospel.

But, those early Christians had something special, something on the inside; they had the help of an *indwelling, sanctifying Savior and the anointing of the Holy Ghost*. And with that equipment they faced a hostile world and all the powers of darkness *but* they won souls to Christ. Within seventy years, there were half a million followers of Jesus and that's a conservative estimate. So, with Holy Ghost power upon them, the 120 increased more than four thousand fold. They were winning souls to Christ. On that first day when that Holy Ghost power fell, three thousand souls were won to Christ. And that's the purpose of the church. If our churches today had a similar anointing of Holy Ghost power, it wouldn't take long to take the whole world for Christ.

No matter how tough it gets or how hard things seem to be, We've got to live according to the will of God and I won't tell you it's easy because it's not. It requires sacrifice - living sacrifice.

When Jesus walked among men, He lived totally in the will of His Father. And there was only one time when He dared think about getting outside of the will of God. But it was **just** a fleeting thought. I thank God for that because we are here today because it was *just* a fleeting thought. It did not last. When Jesus kneeled in the garden to pray, He knew His death was imminent. His hour had come.

He knew the soldiers would be there any minute to get Him. He was on His knees praying and they tell me He was praying so hard that sweat like drops of blood were falling from his brow. You see, ahead of Him was agony, shame, humiliation and a slow, painful death. Crucifixion was the worse possible death sentence that anyone could receive. It was designed to humiliate the person and his family because they hung there in full view of everybody.

My Savior was on His knees, calling out to His Father. He said "Father, if you just remove this cup from me." The cup represented his impending death. Jesus was both human and divine. It was the human side that wanted the cup to pass from him. But then He thought about what else was ahead of Him, something else besides the agony, something else besides the humiliation, something else besides the pain. Ahead of Him was my salvation, your salvation. So the divine side stepped in and said: "*Nevertheless*, not my will, Father, but Your will be done."

Jesus was a holy man, a sinless man who was saying, not my will but thy will. This was a confession that the two wills might not agree. The prayer implies that if the Father's will were done, the Son's will might not be. My will, Jesus is saying, is to avoid the cup. But even as He prays, He knows that the Father's will is that He drink it because our salvation was in the cup.

That's what we have to say, church. When we are tempted to go off in our own directions, after our own desires, we must remember to call ourselves back and say, nevertheless, not my will, Father, but your will be done. Had it not been so, we wouldn't be here today. Had the divine side not taken over, Had God answered and said,

"All right, Son, You don't have to do this, come on back home to glory." Had the Father said that, had Jesus not allowed the divine side to take over, all of us would have been lost - hopelessly lost.

Jesus paid the supreme price and presented Himself a living sacrifice. Christian men and women everywhere, we too, must present our bodies a living sacrifice. We don't have to die on a cross, we only have to do His will and live holy and become vessels of honor for Christ. We just have to yield everything to Him - our body, our soul, our spirit. And when we do this, we will be able to live according to the will of God in this wicked and perverse society. May God bless you.

NO SHAME
IN THE NAME

*For I am not ashamed of the gospel of Christ: for it is
the power of God to salvation to everyone that believes;
to the Jew first, and also to the Greek.*

Romans 1:16

God communicates with us through His Word. And there
are so many ways within His Word that He communicates
with us.

He gave us the Pentateuch - the Law- as a mirror that we
may see ourselves as we really are. And when we see
ourselves through this mirror of the law, it allows us to
understand just how much we need a Savior. He gave us
history that we may learn from the mistakes of others.
When we look at the history, we see what happened to the

Israelites when they were disobedient and rebellious. We saw them punished and taken into captivity time and time again.

He gave us poetry that we may experience the beauty of His divine Word. We find in Psalms some of the most beautifully written poetry. He gave us prophecy that we may know and understand that no matter how things may appear today, Christ is victorious and we with Him.

God gave us a portrait of Jesus Christ masterfully painted through the eyes of Matthew, Mark, Luke and John. He didn't stop there. He gave us warm, personal messages and sound doctrine through the Epistles, most of which came through His bond servant, Paul.

And so we have this Word, this awesome, powerful Word that speaks to us.

One of the Pauline Epistles, Romans, contains the great gospel manifesto for the world. Martin Luther wrote that the Epistle to the Romans is *"the true masterpiece of the New Testament and the very purest gospel, which is well worthy and deserving that a Christian man should not only learn it by heart, word for word, but also that he should daily deal with it as the daily bread of men's souls. It can never be too much or too well read or studied; and the more it is handled, the more precious it becomes, and the better it tastes."* I wholeheartedly agree with Martin Luther.

And someone else said, "If Holy Scripture were a ring and the Epistle to the Romans a cluster of diamonds, then chapter eight would be the center diamond, the sparkling point of the jewels." Again, I agree.

We are talking here about Paul and we find that Paul is writing to Rome. He hasn't visited Rome yet, but he has some Christian friends there. This gospel has spread to Rome. It started in Jerusalem , spread to Samaria and to the outermost parts of the world. It's in Rome now. And there you will find educated, uneducated, great culture as well as the uncultured. But it doesn't matter what's there, Paul knows that this gospel will stand up anywhere.

Question: Can you remember when it was all right to call on the name of Jesus anywhere? Can you remember when prayers at high school graduations and school assemblies all used the name of Jesus freely? Well, today, using the name Jesus is politically incorrect. His name is forbidden in the classrooms and shied away from in public prayer.

Why? Because people are threatened and intimidated by the power of Jesus' name. The entire Epistle of Romans is built on verse 16 of chapter 1.

"For I am not ashamed of the gospel of Christ, for it is the power of God to salvation for everyone who believes." Paul is saying here, there is no shame in the name.

The name *"Jesus"* is the real thing. It means *"Savior"* or "The One who saves." In this world, we have the real things and we have imitators of the real things. There are diamonds and then there are cubic zirconiums. There are Designer bags and there are knock-offs. There is human hair and there is synthetic hair. There are natural flowers and there are silk flowers. We have brand-names and we have something called generics. Generic in the legal sense means not protected by trademark or registration; any food, drug, cosmetic, or product that can be sold without a brand name.

Have you noticed that all prescription drugs that have been on the market a certain period of time have a generic version of the real thing. It's similar to the real thing, but cheaper. That's like a "no-name brand." Remember in the grocery stories some years ago they had the black and white labels. Those were generics - no-name brands.

Today, We have generic gospel. It's not the real thing. And if you are not careful, you may be caught up into something that's not genuine.

We have people who are caught up in cults. It's not the real thing, people. It's an imitation of the real thing. People who are grounded in the faith and people who have been properly instructed in this gospel are not likely to go off running behind some no-name brand religion.

I have heard people say, I left because I wasn't being fed. That offended me because the person who said that never came to the table to be fed. The table is set up and there is a full spread - a five-course meal spread out on the table in Sunday School and they don't show up. There is another table spread out with the Word of God in Bible Study and they don't show up. How can you be fed if you don't sit at the table?

You can't just come on Sunday mornings and expect to understand everything the preacher says in his sermon. When he's talking about regeneration, justification and sanctification, and you haven't been to Sunday school or

Bible study, you don't have a clue about what these terms mean. You can't stop him and say," Hold up, Pastor, will you explain that?" On Sunday mornings, Pastor is a preacher who proclaims the gospel; in Bible Study, he's a teacher who explains the gospel.

Now back to this generic stuff.

I like Ocean Spray Ruby Red & Tangerine juice. But when my money is short, I buy the generic juice. No brand, just the name of the store, similar juice, a whole lot cheaper. But I don't want no generic gospel. I want the gospel of Jesus Christ. It's got to be the gospel that Peter and Paul preached - Jesus Christ, Him crucified, risen and coming again. I want the real gospel.

Today, we have generic prayers. At commencement and baccalaureate services, there were real prayers prayed in the name of Jesus. A few years ago, I attended the Martin Luther King Prayer services at a large church in Palm Beach County. It was multi-racial, multi-cultural, multi-religion. I noticed everyone who prayed came to the podium with written prayers. I don't know if someone had checked them to make sure they were generic, but they sounded pretty much the same. Not wanting to offend anyone, the prayers were bland, lifeless, colorless, odorless and tasteless.

There is power that has been given to us and it's in the gospel but it seems today that many Christians are nonchalant about the greatest power given to man. There are so many of us who don't realize it, don't utilize it, don't appreciate it. Indifference to the gospel appears to be the norm today.

There are those who claim it's bigotry to say Jesus is the only way. They say we're leaving out these other religions - the ones that don't believe in Jesus. Too bad. Jesus says, *"I am the way, the truth and the light. No man comes to the Father except thru me."*

Jesus knew His name would generate controversy and strife. Yet, He said, *"If anyone is ashamed of me and my words in this adulterous and sinful generation, the son of man will be ashamed of him when he comes in his Father's glory with the holy angels."* (Mark 8:38)

Paul in this passage of scripture lets us know that there is no shame in the name. He was not ashamed of the gospel for three reasons:
>   1) He knew where he stood
>   2) He knew where he was going
>   3) He knew his source of real power

1. HE KNEW WHERE HE STOOD - We are living in a time where people are confused about who they are. Male or female, black or white, saved or unsaved, we have a bunch of confused people. It's refreshing to see how the Apostle Paul revealed his identity. Notice how he introduced himself as a bond servant of Jesus Christ. He was linguistically talented, a brilliant student of Gamaliel. If anyone had the right to brag, he did, but he simply introduced himself as a bond servant. That one sentence spelled out Paul's self-perception. He knew where he stood. As a Christian, a healthy, self-perception is not something we achieve, it is a gift of God. Paul was called by God to be an Apostle and a servant. Paul was not ashamed because he knew who he was. Do we know who we are?

People get involved in ministry for a variety of reasons. Some minister out of legalistic motives, trying to earn God's favor. Forget about legalism. You cannot earn God's favor. Others want to serve for the prestige and esteem that leadership brings. Don't expect them to do a task that is not front and center. They have to have high visibility assignments. They've got be seen. Still others are fulfilling their own agendas. They have ulterior motives for everything they do.

Ministry should be done out of a desire to please God. Whether you're singing in the choir or teaching Sunday school or whatever, you should do so not because you were asked to serve, but because you have a sincere desire to be a good servant.

Some people, without realizing it, have poor self-perception. Because of this they worship celebrities, the mega-bucks televangelists. I like to watch some of them, too. But I don't look upon them as stars. I was in class with a lady who worshiped Creflo Dollar. Every night of class, she put two pictures on her desk: one was a picture of what some artist thinks Jesus looks like - blond hair, blue eyes - and the other a picture of Creflo Dollar.

Some of the same Christians who take advice on love and marriage from celebrities, get angry when God's Word is proclaimed. Some people call Madam X or Miss Cleo. People are running to and fro looking for flash and dash, razzle and dazzle when they could stay at home where the real gospel is being proclaimed. You don't have to leave here to get the real gospel. But some people don't want that. They want a feel-good gospel that gives them a temporary high so they can shout and go home and talk about, "Didn't we have church?"

Paul was not ashamed of the Gospel because he knew who he was.

2. HE KNEW WHERE HE WAS GOING - Paul's vision was to go to Rome in God's timing. The average person has little vision for his or her life beyond tomorrow. Your vision for your life has to be God's vision for you. If God's vision is your vision, you don't have to worry because He will accomplish His will on His own timetable.

In the church, the vision is given to the Pastor. It is our duty to get behind the pastor and support the vision of the Pastor. We did that at PHMBC and now our ex-parking lot is a multi-purpose educational building.

Paul also knew why he wanted to go to the Romans. He wanted to see them for mutual encouragement. When encouragement only goes one way, it doesn't last. Do you have people in your lives that are needy to the point that you have to stroke them all the time? Where are they when you need encouragement? Paul knew he wouldn't just meet their needs; he also wanted their support to send him to Spain to continue preaching. They needed each other.

Paul knew his obligation was to preach the Gospel to the world. That's what he meant when he said, "I am a debtor." Paul was obligated to God, but made his payment to the people. Many Christians give lip service, but make no payments. Jesus entrusted the gospel to Paul as a steward. Whatever ministry or resources or gifts God has entrusted to you, you are a "debtor" to God to pass on what He has given you to others. We are debtors and will remain so until everybody has heard this gospel. We have no greater vision in life than to make Jesus known. We have to be able to say there is no shame in the name of Jesus.

3. HE KNEW HIS SOURCE OF REAL POWER - The minute we begin to think we arrived somewhere by our own talent and hard work, look out - we are headed for deep trouble. The entire Protestant Reformation was built on verse 17b. *"The just shall live by faith"* Our lives should be built on this verse. This quote is taken from Habakkuk. 2-4b.

"Faith" in verse 17 covers three different tenses:

1. Faith in the past - you are saved from damnification to glorification when you put your whole trust in Jesus Christ.
2. Faith in the present - which is the daily exercise of trusting God.
3. Faith in the future - when we enter into the gates of heaven.

Salvation not only means putting your trust in Jesus Christ to save you from eternal damnation. It also means to continue exercising faith in Him. God will use you for His kingdom here and now, while providing for all your needs and strengthening you against sin. Then, ultimately, we trust Him to take us to glory. It is all God, from the beginning, the middle, and the end.

I am not ashamed of the gospel of Jesus Christ. And as for me, I know there is *no shame in the name.*

RELAYING THE TORCH OF SALVATION BY FAITH

When I call to remembrance the unfeigned
faith that is in thee which dwelt first in thy grandmother
Lois, and thy mother Eunice; and I am persuaded
that is in thee also.

II Timothy 1:5

There are four key words in this topic:

Relaying - transmitting or conveying or passing on

Torch - a light usually carried in the hand, a source of illumination, enlightenment or guidance

Salvation - deliverance from the power and penalty of sin; redemption

Faith - belief that is not based on proof

Lois and Eunice were two women who impacted the world through teaching and touching a life. They were ordinary women who did extraordinary things. They had the gift of teaching. Ephesians 4:11 says: "*And he gave some, apostles, and some prophets; and some, evangelists; and some, pastors and teachers.*"

They had no formal education; they did not graduate from Teachers College or FAMU or BCU. They had very little culture, very little religious support. There was no synagogue. They had nowhere to worship their God. They didn't have a beautiful sanctuary as we have here today. You see, it took a minimum of twelve Jewish families to have a synagogue. Our ancestors, brought to this country bound and chained in the belly of the ships had nowhere to worship. They had no church. But they had an invisible church. They would "*steal away*" deep into the woods far away from their slave masters hearing and worship God secretly at the risk of being discovered.

Lois and Eunice, two women - marooned in an isolated mountain village in Asia Minor for life. In these mountain villages, life was rough; life was hard.

They had very little hope in life other than to impact the world through a child. They poured their very best into young Timothy - everything they had, and through their teaching, these two women influenced the world.

Lois, the grandmother of Timothy did not marry a Jewish man. Like mother, like daughter, neither did Eunice. The teaching of Timothy fell to Lois and Eunice. What is so outstanding about the fact that the two women taught Timothy?

In the Jewish culture, the fathers were primarily responsible for the instruction of their sons, not the mothers. But Timothy's father was a gentile. In this family, the father could not instruct his son; he did not know how. He wasn't Jewish. But he didn't stand in the way of Timothy's training. Since they couldn't rely on their husbands, Lois and Eunice had to do it themselves. Sometimes, Ladies, the buck stops with us.

Lois and Eunice taught Timothy and they taught him well. How can we say they had the gift of teaching? Every mother has the gift of teaching, because a gracious God knowing the difficulties of life would not give a mother the responsibility of raising a child without giving her the added gift to teach that child. Don't ever say what you can't do. Instead say, *"I can do all things through Christ who strengthens me."* Also, teaching is not measured by how well you instruct, it's measured by how well your child learns. And Timothy learned well. He was an outstanding student. Paul tells us in II Tim 3:14-15 verses:

"But continue thou in the things which thou hast learned and hast been assured of, knowing of whom thou hast learned them; and that from a child thou hast known the holy scriptures, which are able to make thee wise unto salvation through faith which is in Christ Jesus."

There have been some gifted teachers - men and women - who have never seen the inside of a college, some never finished high school and some did not finish elementary school. My mother had only a sixth grade education, but she taught me how to read before I ever set foot in anybody's school. By the time I started school, I was reading the spots off the deer.

God has something on the inside of each of us. We have the capacity to do things that we haven't even dreamed of. Lois and Eunice - two women who impacted the world had a little relay system going on.

I'm sure you remember the relay races when we were children. The first person would run a certain distance and pass the stick to the next person and she would run her distance and pass it to the person who ran to the finish line. We have seen these races in the Olympics; not only must you run fast, but a smooth passing of the baton is necessary to ensure a win. In order to get Timothy to the finish line, there was a race going on. And that race was for Timothy's salvation.

Lois ran the first lap and taught Timothy all she knew. She passed the torch to Eunice and she taught all she knew. Eunice passed the torch to Paul and he ran for the finish line. He taught Timothy how to relay the message of salvation by faith to others. He taught him to be a good pastor. The ultimate goal in this race was the salvation of Timothy. They made it. What about us? Saints, this life is a race. We only go around one time and this is **not** a practice run.

Ladies, after you have reared your children, and you are enjoying your retirement, how would you like for your life to be remembered? What will **you** remember about your life? Your first home? Your first car? Your first job?

Or will you remember you accepted Christ as your personal Savior and received the priceless gift of Salvation?

Without a doubt, the greatest legacy you can leave in life is a child who knows and lives the Word of God. Whether you like it or not, your contribution to life will be measured by the contribution of your children after you're gone. And if you think you are home free because you didn't give birth to any, you are wrong. All of these children are ours. Help a young mother who is struggling. Assist a grandmother who is trying to raise her grands. This torch has to be relayed from one generation to another.

In this race God will send some help. He will not leave you alone. He sent Lois and Eunice some help.

1. **They had each other**. Sisters in Christ, we have each other. If things get a little hard for you, you can cry on my shoulder, because tomorrow it may be my time to cry on your shoulder. Sisters, we can help each other, but we need to bond together. I can't help but notice that men have a special kind of friendship. They can have arguments, high volume discussions, disagreements and still remain friends. We can have one little argument and don't speak to each other for years. Sometimes, ten years later we can't remember why we don't like sister Sue. We just know we don't like her. We need to stop that. God doesn't like it.

How can you love God whom you have never seen and yet not love the sister sitting next to you in the pew on Sunday mornings? We should be sensitive to each other's needs. It's important that we respect, trust and love each other. Well, you may say it was different with Lois and Eunice. They were blood relatives. Well, so are we. Because we believe that Jesus is the Christ, the son of the Living God, we have the right to be called children of God. That makes us sisters, not *by* blood, but *under* the blood.

2. They had the Bible. Even though they were the human instruments to bring Timothy to salvation, what they taught - the Word of God- was responsible for his salvation. Ladies, this Bible is life's instruction manual. It's a how-to book. It teaches us how to live godly and we, in turn, can influence someone else to live godly just as Lois and Eunice did. And I'll tell you something about godly living. It's just like the measles, **You can't give it unless you've got it.** This Bible is bound on one side by eternity, it's bound on the other side by eternity and all in between, God is working it out. From Genesis to Revelation, everything you need to know about godly living is in it. Use it freely, use it daily.

3. Paul helped them. Paul arrived on the scene when Timothy was approximately 16 years old. He may have been the one to lead Timothy to Christ, but the foundation had already been laid by Lois and Eunice. They enjoyed salvation as Jews, but when Paul preached Jesus Christ to them, they believed in Jesus Christ and were converted.

We don't have a Paul, but we have our spiritual leaders - our Pastors. They're sent by God to teach us and ladies, we need to listen. Christ is the head of the church, but the pastor is the shepherd of this flock. Just as the tail cannot wage the dog, the sheep cannot lead the shepherd. Paul know Timothy would have obstacles. First of all, he was a young man. Older pastors have to endure fiery darts, but young pastors have to dodge flaming arrows. So Paul taught Timothy all that he needed to know about the operation of the church - creed, conduct, responsibility of leaders. He taught him how to fight the good fight.

Paul himself had met Christ on Damascus Road. His life was forever changed. Before his encounter with Christ, Paul, formerly Saul of Tarsus, persecuted Christians. But just **one touch**, that's all it took, one touch from the master turned his life around. Ladies, Have you been touched by the Master? Do you have anything to pass on? Is your life filled with joy, peace, love, faith? Are your steps ordered in His Word? Are you the beneficiary of God's Amazing Grace?

I want to share this story with you.

There was an auction going on in town. This auctioneer was superb. He could sell anything. He would hold up an item and sell it to the highest bidder. But the last item was hardly worth the auctioneer's time. It was a violin - old, dusty, battered and scarred - but he held it up with a smile. "What am I bid? Who will start the bidding for Me? Can I get ten dollars?" No response. "Can I get five dollars?" No response.

This had never happened to the auctioneer before. He was always able to sell every item. It seemed no one wanted the violin. It was old, not in very good condition. He tried one more time. "Can I get two dollars? Do I hear two dollars? Anybody. Do I hear two dollars?" There was no response.

The auctioneer proceeded to cancel the item and close the auction. But from the back of the room, and elderly gentleman walked up to the front, picked up the violin, wiped away the dust, tightened the strings and started to play. The room became very still. All sound ceased. He was playing "Amazing Grace". What a soul-stirring sound. You could almost hear the words:

> *Amazing Grace, How sweet the sound, that saved a wretch like me.*
> *I once was lost, but now I'm found, was blind but now I see.*

All across that room people were affected. Ice-cold hearts started to melt. Troubles seemed so distant. Tears were flowing all over the place. He kept playing:

> *T'was grace that taught my heart to fear, And grace my fears relieved;*
> *How precious did that grace appear, The hour I first believed.*

He was a master violinist. He played on:

> *Through many dangers, toils, and snares, I have already come.*
> *T'was grace that brought me safe thus far, and grace will lead me on home."*

He finished playing, gently laid the violin down and walked out of the room. It was a couple of minutes before the auctioneer could compose himself, because he was silently thanking God for His amazing grace. Finally, he resumed the auction. He said, "What am I bid for the old violin. $1,000 and who'll make it 2. $2,000 and who'll make it three? $3,000 once, $3000 twice, and going and gone."

The auction was over. As everyone left, someone from the crowd approached the auctioneer and said, "Mr auctioneer, can I ask you a question? At first nobody wanted the violin and then in the end everybody wanted the violin. Mr. Auctioneer, what changed the value of the violin? What made the difference? The auctioneer said, "The difference was the *touch* of the Master's hand."

Ladies, as I close, I say to you today, you are in a position to touch lives and make a difference. You are in a position to impact the world and affect greatness by passing the torch of - *salvation by faith*. Salvation. What a precious gift. It was not by your works. You don't have salvation because you sing in the choir on Sunday mornings. You don't have this gift because you serve on the usher board. Oh, no, that's not why you have the gift of salvation. It's because you believe in Jesus Christ, the Son of the living God. It's because you put your faith in Him.

You have salvation because you believe in the One who walked the dusty streets of Galilee, healing the sick, giving sight to the blind, raising the dead, and feeding the hungry. You have salvation because you believe in the One who was by your side as you sat by the bedside of your dying loved one. He was the one who comforted you as you cried all night long over wayward children and unpaid bills.

He is the One who calmed you by reminding you that He will neither leave you nor forsake you. Salvation is a precious gift. It is a gift wrapped in sacrifice and tied with blood. Jesus, my Savior, came that we might have this gift. This Jesus, my Savior, was born in a stranger's barn, died on a man-made cross and was buried in a borrowed tomb.

But that's not the end of the story. This Jesus, my Savior, arose with all power in his hands. This Jesus, giver of salvation - He's everything for everybody, everywhere, every time and every way. He is God. He is faithful. I am His and He is mine. Jesus, giver of salvation, He is the keeper of Creation and the Creator of all.

Jesus, My Savior. Is He your Savior? If he's your Savior, hold that torch of 'salvation by faith' high and light the way for someone stumbling in the dark trying to find the path of righteousness. Be a light, ladies. Carry the torch and when it is time, pass it on.

May God bless you.

RIGHT PLACE, RIGHT TIME

*For if thou altogether holdest thy peace at this time,
then shall there enlargement and deliverance arise to
the Jews from another place; but thou and thy father's
house shall be destroyed: and who knoweth whether
thou art come to the kingdom for such a time as this?*

Esther 4:14

QUESTION: What if all African-Americans were
sentenced to die ten months from today? And what if you
were the only person who could save the race? How
would you feel? Would you feel proud or pressured?
Would you be courageous or cowardly? Or would you be
just plain scared to death? Stay tuned to find out how one
woman handled just such a situation as this.

There are two books of the Bible that bear the name of women: Ruth and Esther. Ruth became the ancestress of the Messiah. Esther saved the people so that the Messiah could come.

The book of Esther is about the upsets in human history and the final triumph of God's chosen people; it is about the courage to commit to God in treacherous times; it is about being in the right place at the right time. It's about breaking the silence. It's about the Divine Providence of God. And although His name is not mentioned, every page is full of God; He hides himself behind every word.

Even when we cannot see God, He is there. God never loses sight of his people. Even when they were taken into captivity, God did not abandon them. He followed them in their captivity into Babylon.

When the prophets were silent and the temple closed, God was standing guard. When the kings and the earth feasted and forgot, God remembered and with His hand he wrote their doom or moved their hand to work His glory.

To bring you up to our focus verse, this is what had taken place.

The Jews were in captivity in Persia under King Ahasuerus otherwise known as Xerzes. The queen is Vashti. The king was a proud man. It was important that he impress his nobles and military leaders with his wealth and power. After winning a major battle, the king threw a victory party to end all parties. Food was succulently delicious and the wine flowed as freely as water in the Mississippi River. The celebration went on for days.

The queen was entertaining the women separately in her apartment. According to the custom of the day, women did not mix socially with the men. The men had their party going on and the women had theirs.

The king partied and partied. In the process, he got drunk. Alcohol can cause one to do ugly things. It's been known to wreck marriages, ruin bodies and mind, tear up families, and shatter careers.

The king in his drunkenness decided to parade Vashti before all his drunken guest. She was summoned to appear before the King. Vashti, being a woman of modesty as well as majesty, refused to be paraded for all eyes to look upon her as a "thing of beauty", a possession, a toy, a show thing. She refused to come. No Persian women would permit this. It was an insult to her womanhood. Drunkenness had outraged the most sacred rules of Oriental etiquette.

Vashti, like many women then and now, had one too many disrespectful and insensitive demands placed upon her. I can imagine, like Fannie Lou Hamer, the passionate civil rights leader, Vashti "was sick and tired of being sick and tired." And so, this makes her one of the first woman activist portrayed in ancient culture. Queen Vashti decided to step out and speak up on a woman's right to say "no."

This was unheard of. For a woman to say "no" to the king, even if she is his wife, was shocking. There was no 'women's lib' in Persia. This created a problem for the king, an embarrassment.

This made him a laughingstock, humiliated in front of his men. His ego was bruised. People say hell has no fury like a woman scorned. You haven't seen anything until you've seen a man with a bruised ego. When the ego is bruised, it releases a powerful poison that makes people do all sorts of things they'd never do if they were humble and submitted to the Lord.

Men, you have to realize that modesty is the crown jewel of a woman and you are supposed to protect this jewel of womanhood. How could the king expect this of Vashti. The king, in order to save face, had to take action. If he couldn't rule his wife, he couldn't rule a kingdom. And the other men would have trouble out of their wives, too. They wanted him to do something about Vashti. He decided to put her away as queen.

The search was on to find another queen. One woman after another was brought before him. He didn't find anybody suitable until he laid eyes on Esther. When he saw her, he knew this was his new queen. Esther, a young, Jewish orphan raised by Mordecai, was lifted to the status of Queen of Persia. Of course, Mordacai had warned her to keep her racial identity a secret.

Meanwhile, several things have happened. Mordecai has saved the king's life and it was written in the book of records. But there was a shadow across this beautiful picture of the young Jewish girl who became queen. There is always a spoiler in the mix. Haman was a wicked man who had been elevated to the position of chief minister to the king - his right-hand man. This high honor caused him to get "the big head." He was puffed up with vanity and inflated with pride.

The trouble started when Esther's uncle, Mordecai, who sat at the gate, refused to bow to Haman. This made him so mad that he talked the king into issuing a decree that would exterminate all Jews just ten months away. Just think, all Jews must die because one Jew failed to bow to Haman.

How evil can you be?

Mordecai got wind of this evil plot cooked up by Haman. He sent word to Esther that she must go before the king and plead the cause for the Jews. It was the custom that anyone appearing before the king without permission would be executed unless the king extended his scepter. Esther knew she would die. So Esther sent word back to Mordecai saying, "I can't do that. I will lose my life. If I go before the King uninvited, I will die. He hasn't summoned me in thirty days. I'm Sorry."

This brings us to the focus verse. From the living Bible, it says, "If you keep quiet at a time like this, God will deliver the Jews from some other source, but you and your relatives will die; what's more, who can say but that God has brought you into the palace for just such a time as this?"

Mordecai wanted Esther to understand that all the Jews would be killed, including her. Being the queen would not spare her life.

Esther had to think about that. And so after agonizing over the dilemma, she answers the challenge of Mordecai. She chose a course at terrible danger to herself for the sake of her people. She said, "I'll go before the king, and if I die, I die." Esther faced death, but she was too anointed, too appointed to die. She had a purpose in life. She was in the right place at the right time.

There are times when we have to stick our neck out, times when we have to go out on a limb and stand up for something. There are times when we can no longer be content and stand back in the safety of the shadows. We learn from Esther that even a person not noted for courage can rise to the occasion. We can *act* against our normal character and *live* beyond our normal potential. There is a time when we have to stand up and speak out.

God prepares us for emergencies. And if we fail, that's not a sin; to have no faith, is a sin. There is a time to act. When God speaks, we must act. And so Esther decided, I have to do this. But there is something that has to be done before we step out on a task such as this. Esther says, "Gather up the people. Tell them to fast for three days. Don't eat anything. Don't drink anything. And I and my handmaidens will so the same." There was no mention of praying. But where there is spiritual fasting, there is praying. I just have to believe, that somewhere, somebody was praying.

The beauty of Esther is that she wasn't spoiled by her lofty position. She remained humble. That's a lesson for us to learn. Some of us become so high and mighty when we reach a certain status that we become untouchable and unreachable. We forget where we came from, and who brought us.

Once Esther accepted the terrible task, she carried it out with courage. It was a daring act to appear before the king uninvited, but she had to take a chance. She was still afraid, yet she faced her fears and determined to act anyway. She did what she had to do realizing she could not control the outcome.

When she was received by the king, she gave it everything she had. She used her resources. She got dressed in her royal apparel, put on her crown, and her sweetest perfume and strolled into the palace with an air of confidence. I'm sure she was looking her very best. She waited to be recognized. Ladies, we all have resources. We need to know what our resources are, when to use them and how to use them. This sister had her act together.

Esther knew the king's weakness was good living. He loved to eat, so she invited him to a banquet. She also invited Haman, the enemy. The Bible says the Lord will prepare a table before us in the presences of our enemies. That's what Esther did. When the king asked her what she wanted, she told him. "I want to live. I want my people to live. I and my people have been sentenced to death ten months from now. You see, my King, I am a Jew."

Esther had never revealed her racial identity to the King until now. She begged for her life and the life of her people. The king wanted to know, "Who sentenced you to die?" She said, "Haman, your right-hand man." Haman was trapped. He was hung on the same gallows he had prepared for Mordecai and Mordecai was elevated to the place of honor next to the king.

When it was all over, Esther's people were saved from extermination. She realized Mordecai was right. She had come to her royal position for such a time as this. She was in the right place at the right time.

It's good to know that we are not trapped by our weaknesses. God uses us as we are, placing us where we can serve him and others. If the time comes when we must step out of character to do his work, the Lord will give us the grace to live beyond our capabilities.

We weren't just called to sit in the sanctuary in our pretty white dresses on Sunday mornings. We cannot afford to be part of the silent majority. As fervently as we pray, we need also to speak out in action so others can hear. We need to pray and act under God's direction. We have to pray without ceasing and be about our duty of witnessing and lifting up the name of Jesus.

Sisters, we have been called for such a time as this. If not now, when? If not you, who? We are not saved to wait for some distant future. We are saved to be responsible for those around us right here and right now. The greatest need in the world today is that the world be led to Christ. This may not be popular topic of conversation, but Jesus is still what the world needs. Who is going to lift the name of Jesus if we don't do it?

It's time to do away with the "me, myself and I' mentality. We are called to let the whole world know about this Christ whose name we bear.

And that world includes the Hamans of the world. It includes the barons of the drug trade, the victims of HIV affliction, the lost world of sickness and distress. My sisters, we have to become so totally involved in the world's cries for help, so committed to serve that never again will our babies be found in dumpsters, or slammed against the hood of a car and dumped into the water. We must become so involved that never again will our children be lost and no one knows where they are. We must be so involved that racism, sexism, violence and corruption will become bad memories instead of stark reality.

Sisters we are called to make a difference in the world. We must become agents of change. God challenges us so that we will have the courage to transform our classrooms and playgrounds from battlegrounds to parks of peace. We should not have to live in a world where people are killed or abducted just trying to shop at the local mall or slaughtered on a college campus or gunned down while having lunch in a Wendy's restaurant.

We are walking on perilous pathways. There is no room for complacency. We are called to be like Esther, called to lay aside our fears and make a bold step for Christ. What other time in history has there been such a great opportunity to serve?

Sisters, my questions to you today are: When the Lord returns, will we be doing what He expects to find us doing? Are we feeding the hungry, clothing the naked, housing the homeless, loving the children, lifting up the name of Jesus? Why are we here at such a time as this? What are we doing in the kingdom? What are we doing in God's name?

It doesn't take a lot of people to accomplish his purpose. He can use one person. If He wants to start a revolution,

He can do it with one person. If He wants to start a new nation, He can use an Abraham. If He wants to overthrow an Egyptian Pharaoh with 600 chosen chariots, He can use a Moses. If He wants to add a Caananite thread to the lineage of Christ, he will go get a prostitute named Rahab out of the red-light district. The fate of the captive Jews rested on the shoulders of one woman.

Sometimes it comes down to one person. And you may be that one person, the one who is in the right place at the right time.

Sisters, who knows? You may have come to Pleasant Heights for such a time as this. It doesn't matter about your past. You may have been misused and abused. You may have trusted someone who turned on you and broke your heart. But God has kept you. You are here today because He sustained you. You didn't make it based on your own strength. You didn't make it because you are so wise or so smart. You made it because God's amazing grace kept you.

God knows who we all are. He knew us before we were formed in our mother's womb. He recognizes the possibility of what we can become. He has a plan for my life and a plan for your life. He sees our potential. And he knows that our potential has been bound by our history.

As I close, I say to you: Hidden inside each of us is a great woman who can do great things in the name of Jesus. He wants us to be set free. He wants the potential in us to be unleashed so we can become the person He created us to be. And I don't have to tell you God didn't create no junk.

This story of Esther was a picture of God's divine providence. Because of the obedience of a little Jewish maiden girl who became queen, the Jews were *saved* and the way was *paved* for the Messiah to come.

And He came, church. He came. He walked the dusty streets of Galilee. He ministered, He fed the hungry, gave sight to the blind, healed the sick, raised the dead. And then He suffered and died that we might live. And two weeks from today, we will celebrate Resurrection Sunday. I am glad Esther was at the right place at the right time and Ladies, we, too, are at the right place at the right time.

GOD'S LITTLE "BIG MAN"

And Jabez called on the God of Israel, saying, Oh that thou wouldest bless me indeed, and enlarge my coast, and that thine hand might be with me, and that thine hand might be with me, and that thou wouldst keep me from evil, that it may not grieve me.
And God granted him that which he requested.

I Chronicles 4:10

I am constantly amazed at the Word of God. It is inexhaustible. The more I read, the more I study, the more I realize how much I don't know. There are always new truths to be discovered, new concepts to be explored. We all have our favorite passages - time-honored passages- that we love to read.

Sometimes we miss "diamonds" tucked away in a corner of the Bible that we very seldom read. This morning we have such a scripture. We have our favorite characters in scripture. There is Joseph and his amazing technicolor coat. There is Daniel who won a battle with the lions without lifting a finger. We have David who slew the giant with a slingshot and five smooth stones. There is the Apostle Paul, an amazingly brilliant man with an unequaled zeal for the gospel of Jesus Christ. There is Esther, Noah, John the Baptist and many others. But this morning I want you to turn to the first book of the Chronicles.

Chapter one through nine has nothing but names and more names, some too hard to pronounce.

Chapter 1 - the sons of Adam
Chapter 2 - the sons of Israel
Chapter 3 - the sons of David
Chapter 4 - the sons of Judah and so forth and so on.

Who would spend a lot of time reading a bunch of names you can't even pronounce and you would never remember. But wait a minute. Let's look at chapter four. It appears that the historian - when he was giving the names - had a thought and he broke the chain of genealogy to tell us about a man. And he tells us about this man in just two verses.

He broke up this genealogy to give us these verses. And after these verses, he went right back to the genealogy of the sons of Judah. This is a man that we never hear anything about anywhere else in the Bible. He may not be a big man like Abraham or Moses or Noah, but we can call him *God's Little Big Man*. There is something that we can learn from him, something that can change our lives.

It is such a little prayer, just one sentence with four parts. But it's such a powerful prayer. This little prayer reveals that our Father wants to give us so much more than we have ever thought to ask for. Jabez doesn't dominate the old testament like Moses or David. He doesn't light up the Book of Acts like Peter or Paul. But the tiny little prayer that he prayed has the capacity to change our lives. This prayer can expand our opportunities to make a difference in the lives of those around us. So let's take a closer look at this prayer.

1. Oh that you would bless me indeed.

What does the word "bless" mean? This word has been overused, misused and abused. It's become so common - it's like saying "have a nice day" or "God bless you." Even my two year old grandson says "bless you" when someone sneezes. We have really taken the word lightly. When you ask God to bless you, you're not asking him to do something for you that you can do for yourself. You're asking him for supernatural favor.

What do we know about Jabez?

As far as we know, he lived in southern Israel and was born into the tribe of Judah. His story begins with his name. His mother called him Jabez saying, *I bore him in pain*. Jabez in Hebrew means *pain*. Another meaning

could be, *he causes or will cause pain*. That doesn't sound like a great start in life. Having given birth to two children, I know that babies arrive with a certain amount of pain. But there was something about Jabez's birth that was unusual. So much so that his mother chose to memorialize it in her son's name. Why? We don't know for sure.

Only God knew for sure. Jabez overcame his name. He had grown up hearing about the God of Israel who had freed his forefathers from slavery. He had rescued them from powerful enemies and established them in the land of plenty.

No matter the circumstances of your birth, you can always rise above. The fact that we were born black meant that we were born with a certain amount of pain. We were born with the prospect of an uncertain future. We were born knowing that we had to be superstars just to be considered average. But that's ok because we were also born with the promises of an Almighty God. We can overcome the circumstances of our birth and that's what Jabez did. Jabez prayed, *"Oh that you would bless me indeed."* Indeed means a whole lot. It's like saying, "Lord, bless me a whole lot, not just a little bit, Lord, but a whole lot."

When we ask for God's blessing, we're not asking for more of what we could get for ourselves. We're crying out for the wonderful, unlimited goodness that only God has the power to give us.

In proverbs 10:22. *"The Lord's blessing is our greatest wealth; all our work adds nothing to it."* Notice Jabez left it up to God to decide what the blessings would be and where, when, and how Jabez would receive them.

In the prayer, Jabez is not asking for the ordinary food, clothing and shelter. He is asking for the extraordinary blessing. That's when the word "indeed" is added. God's blessing is limited not by his resources or his willingness to give; but by our failure. Jabez was blessed because he refused to let any obstacle, any person or any opinion to get in his way. God's nature is to bless. I thank God for recording Jabez's story in the Bible because it proves that it's not who we are, or what our parents decided for us that counts. What counts is knowing who you want to be and asking for it.

So through this simple prayer you can change your future. You can change what happens one minute from now.

The second line from this prayer:
ENLARGE MY TERRITORY

When you say enlarge my territory, or coasts or boundaries, you're asking God to enlarge your life so that you can make a greater impact for Him. We can see from Jabez's prayer, he is not asking for more real estate. He wanted more influence. He wanted more responsibility. He wanted more opportunity to make a mark for God. He wanted every thing that God put under his care to be enlarged.

When you pray this prayer, you're asking God - "God, everything that you've entrusted in my care, take it and enlarge it."

EXAMPLES:

1. MINISTER - God increase my opportunity to minister

to those who are lost that I may lead them to Christ.

2. BUSINESS EXECUTIVE - God, increase my business. It's ok to ask that because He has entrusted that business to me. That's my territory. He's waiting on me to ask. I can use that to make a significant impact on my community.

3. INVESTMENT BROKER - increase the value of my investment portfolios.

4. MOTHER - Add to my family, favor my key relationships. Multiply for your glory the influence of my household.

Your household may be the model that other people look at and say when I marry and have a family I want to be like that family. I want to be like that mother. Your home, if that's your prayer, is the single most powerful arena on earth to change a life for God. You can rear a child that one day may be a great evangelist that saves souls for Christ. You may raise a great doctor that may one day save many lives. You as a mother have an opportunity to change the world by the way you run your household.

5. TEACHER -an overwhelming opportunity to affect the lives of young people. I think of Marva Collins who proved that when you show children that you believe in them you can influence them to perform way beyond their normal capabilities.

What do you want God to do for you? What is the territory God has entrusted with you? It's different for each of us.

THAT YOUR HAND WOULD BE WITH ME

You've asked for this increased territory. You have an armload of God's blessings, marched into new territory... and stumbled into overwhelming circumstances. You've received a level of blessings you didn't even know was possible. A little anxiety sets in. Now you wonder if you're in over your head. You don't know if you can handle it.

Some people fall at this point because they feel out of control. Maybe that new business opportunity threatens to outrun your experience and resources. But if God blesses you, He will also equip you.

THAT YOU WOULD KEEP ME FROM EVIL

Picture the Roman gladiator in the arena with the roaring lion. One of them would not get out alive. Either the lion or the gladiator will die. There are times when you can't afford to come in second.

Notice that Jabez did not pray "keep me *through* evil." Rather, keep me from evil. The best way to avoid being eaten by the lion is not to enter the arena in the first place.

AND GOD GRANTED HIM HIS REQUEST.

My challenge to you is to make this prayer a daily part of your life as I have done. From the time I started to pray this prayer, the opportunities started to come. At times they came so fast, I had to ask God to give me time to catch up on the opportunities he opened up for me.

> 1. Pray the Jabez prayer every morning and keep a record of your daily prayer by marking off a calendar or a chart you make especially for the

purpose.

2. Tape a copy of the prayer in your Bible or on your bathroom mirror or some other place where you'll be reminded of your new vision. But no matter how many places you put this prayer, nothing will happen except what you believe will happen.

3. Tell one other person of your commitment to your new prayer habit, and ask her to check up on you. This will keep you accountable.

4. Begin to keep a record of changes in your life, especially the divine appointments and new opportunities you can relate directly to the Jabez prayer. You will be amazed.

5. Start praying the Jabez prayer for your family, friends, and local church. This is beyond a doubt a powerful prayer.

It's OK to ask God for the best He has in mind for you. I ask God to increase my opportunities to use the gift He has given me to help others and to glorify Him. Step up to God's best for you. Remember, He's waiting to bless you. I am a living witness that this prayer works.

May God forever bless you.

Raising the Standards Through Prayer, Discipline and Service

*So shall they fear the name of the Lord from the west,
and his glory from the rising of the sun. When the
enemy shall come in like a flood, the Spirit of the Lord
shall lift up a standard against him.*

Isaiah 59:9

Women of Saint James, I commend you for your very comprehensive and timely theme. My problem is that there is so much we can say about this theme. We can turn this into a full-scale workshop; however, we only have a few minutes. The four key words: standard, prayer, discipline, and service have a combined total of 67 definitions. Where do we start?

The "b" clause of Isa 59:19 tells us that when the enemy comes to overwhelm us, we have the assurance that the

Spirit of the Lord shall lift up a standard against the enemy. A standard in this Scripture has military connotations. It is the banner at the head of a marching army.

Even today the word standard has military meanings among it's 28 definitions. In the days of Jeremiah and Isaiah the term standard indicated that God was going to deal with the enemy.

Today, we too, have an enemy to deal with. Our enemy comes in many forms: poverty, ignorance, hatred, internet pornography, pedophiles and violence. That's just a few of them. We now face overwhelming problems in our community. We know we have a battle ahead of us. It is going to take much *prayer*, total *discipline* and unselfish *service*.

There are several definitions for *standard*. Whatever we choose to think that standard means - whether we are marching against an enemy or raising the level of education, housing, health or employment - we know one thing for sure; there is an enemy facing us.

Just take a look at the content of the newspapers and evening news.

"Three year old shot and killed in apartment complex in Riviera Beach."

"Two Black males killed in drive-by shooting in Riviera Beach."

"Toddler killed in hit and run accident in Riviera Beach."

"Three of four failing elementary schools are in Riviera Beach."

"Black male shot 7 times on Avenue S in Riviera Beach."

Every now and then Riviera Beach gets a little relief and the bad news comes from West Palm Beach. "Killings occur again on Palm Beach Lakes Blvd."

Our churches are situated in communities where there are many such problems. Is there work to be done? Yes. Are there standards to be raised? Yes. Is it going to take prayer, service and discipline? Yes, it is.

When you raise a standard, you are raising a banner that says you are going to war against situations, problems, conflicts in your home, schools, neighborhoods, country. When Jeremiah and Isaiah mentioned raising a standard, war was imminent. We are in a war now. We are in a fight for the lives of our children. We are in a fight for our young men dying violently in the street and alleys of Riviera and West Palm Beach.

We are in a fight to raise health care standards. The number of African-Americans without health insurance is mind boggling. Effort must be made to enable all uninsured Americans to secure health insurance.

Discipline - We understand that there is more than one meaning of this word. One means to chastise and correct. But today we mean the kind of discipline required to have a strong, consistent, effective prayer life. Our effort cannot be hit and miss or wishy-washy. James says, *"The* *effective, fervent prayer of a righteous man availeth much."*

We are in a fight to raise standards in our educational system. A few years ago the FCAT was implemented in our state public schools. One year, there were 4 failing elementary failing schools, three of them in Riviera Beach. Since that time scores have improved. That sent out a message, not necessarily the correct message. Some would assume that our children are slow and can't learn. That's not true. We have children who are spending too much time in front of the TV looking at BET and MTV, too much time on the internet in these chat rooms and Myspace.com, too much time playing violent, electronic games.

This problem does not lie solely on the backs of the educators. I don't care how much money you pump into the educational system, until there is parental involvement, things will not greatly improve.

There are some children who will not get this parental involvement. There are some children being raised by children because babies have had babies. Grandmothers, Grand aunts - you have to take up the slack. Some of our children are falling through the cracks. The dropout rate is huge. Many of those who reach graduation day are walking out of high school with certificates of attendance rather than diplomas. This does not have to be.

Let me tell you about one woman who did not leave the education of her children totally up to the school system. I talk about her all the time even though I've never met her and will probably never meet her. Her name is Sonya.

Sonya loves her boys, Curtis and Benjamin. And just like us, just like any mother, she wanted the best for them. But sometimes, circumstances change and in 1959, life threw Sonya a curve ball.

Her husband left her with two little boys to raise alone. They moved to Boston to live with relatives for a year. And then they returned to Detroit's inner city. The inner-city is tough. Only the strong survive. Sonya was thrown into a world of poverty with only a third-grade education. She worked hard as a domestic to provide for her boys.

When they returned to Detroit in 1960, her sons attended the pre-dominantly white Higgins Elementary School, and found themselves at the bottom of the class with the danger of being labeled "slow learners." Benjamin was called "class dummy." And because he was taunted by classmates and ignored by teachers, he became convinced of his own stupidity. But Sonya said to the system, "Don't label my children."

Sonya was determined. She took the boys to the library and got a library card for them. She made them read two books a week and write a book report. She couldn't read the report, but the boys didn't know that. They did as they were told. Sonya turned off the TV while they read. She was relentless. By reading books, Benjamin began to acquire the knowledge that would send him to the head of the class, earn the respect of his classmates and teachers and convince him of his self-worth and potential.

Ben went from being "class dummy" to the top of his class because he had an ordinary Christian mother who would not sit idly by and allow her children to be labeled.

Ben would go on to become a world famous surgeon, the head of Neurosurgery at John Hopkins Hospital. Yes, Sonya was an ordinary woman in the eyes of some, but she was extraordinary in the eyes of God. Did she help anyone other than her immediate family? Yes, she did. Every time Dr. Ben Carson saves a life, we can say "thank you" to Sonya Carson. The life he saved could be a future president or a scientist who finds a cure for cancer.

The discipline of going to the prayer closet has revealed an important truth: Prayer is the key to moving our lives in a successful direction. The idea of investing in your prayer life may seem potentially boring and repetitive, but it is hugely rewarding. We cannot begin to think that we can remotely raise *standards* without a successful prayer life. In whatever capacity we choose to serve, we have to pray without ceasing.

One person can make a difference. You can talk to one young man on the streets. If you know him, you have some influence on him. You can sit him down and talk to him. There might not be an immediate change, but you have planted a seed, a thought that may come back to him at the right time, at the very time he is getting ready to get into something from which he will never recover. He will remember that you said to him, "Son, you can do better than this, There is a better life for you than the one on the streets. Think about your future, son."

We've had young men stop by our house and say to my husband, "Mr. Knighton, I want you to know that I have a job now. I'm not out on the streets now. I stopped smoking that stuff." It's such a good feeling to know that somebody listened. We can't save everybody. Some will not listen. Some will end up incarcerated for long periods of time. Some will end up dead. But we can't give up. We must try. And when that one person turns his life around, it is time for rejoicing. The fight goes on.

Jesus rejoices over the one that is saved. Sometimes the only thing a young person needs is to know that people care.

Prayer. The main ingredient in your theme is prayer. There is one thing we can be sure of, God accepts our prayers. Some tend to think they are not eloquent enough. But listen to this:

God looks not at the **oratory** of your prayers, how *elegant* they may be; nor at the **geometry** of your prayers, how *long* they may be; nor at the **arithmetic** of your prayers, how *many* they may be; nor at the **logic** of your prayers, how *methodical* they may be; but He looks at the sincerity of your prayers.

We are here today, sitting in the St James Baptist Church, because God has kept us for such a time as this. He has sustained us. We didn't make it on our own strength. We didn't make it because we are wise or perfect. We made it because God's amazing grace kept us.

Let's not put limits on ourselves. Neither education nor the lack thereof, economic status, or circumstances of birth should limit us. The fact that I was born in a row house on the edge of a bean-field in a migrant camp can not and will not limit me. The world may look at me and see nothing, but God looks at me and sees His creation.

My God planted greatness in me just like He did in Esther

of the Bible, just like He did in Sonya, just like He did in all of you.

Ladies, it does not take an army to accomplish God's purposes. If He wants to start a revolution, He can use one person. If He wants to start a new nation, He can use an Abraham. If He wants to overthrow an Egyptian Pharaoh, He can use a Moses. If He wants to add a Canaanite thread to the lineage of Christ, He can pull a prostitute named Rahab from the red-light district. If He wants to save captive Jews from extermination. He can use an Esther.

Sometimes it comes down to one person. And each of us in here today has a purpose. In raising standards, there is a job for each of us to do. You may say, 'the job is too big, it's like eating an elephant. And how do you eat an elephant?" One bite at a time.

If we are to raise standards, we have to pull off these pretty white dresses, roll up our sleeves and go to work. Although it seems that the situation is out of control, remember Isaiah said, " *when the enemy comes to overwhelm us, the Spirit of the Lord will raise a standard against him*."

As I close, Let me share this poem with you about prayer because that is what is going to keep us. Prayer is going to give us the strength to keep on keeping on. It is our means of communicating with God. The poem is entitled "Traveling on my Knees" by Sandra Goodwin.

> Last night I took a journey to a land across the seas:
> I did not go by plane or boat; I traveled on my knees.
> I saw so many people there in deepest depths of sin.

But Jesus told me I should go, that there were souls to win.
But I said, "Jesus, I can't go and work with such as these."
He answered quickly, "Yes, you can by traveling on your knees."
He said, "You pray; I'll meet the need, you call and I will hear;
Be concerned about lost souls, of those both far and near."
And so I tried it, knelt in prayer, gave up some hours of ease;
I felt the Lord right by my side while traveling on my knees.
As I prayed on I saw souls saved and twisted bodies healed,
And saw God's workers' strength renewed while laboring on the fields.
I said, "Yes, Lord, I have a job, my desire Thy will to please;
I can go and answer your call by traveling on my knees."

Keep praying church. God bless you.

A FAITH THAT FOSTERS PIONEERING SPIRITS

Now faith is the substance of things hoped for, the evidence of things not seen.

Hebrews 11:1

Every 45 seconds, an American child is abused or neglected. Every 62 seconds, an American teenager has a baby. Every 6 minutes, an African-American child is arrested for drug abuse. Every 35 minutes an African-American is arrested for drunken driving. Every 33 minutes, an African American child is killed or injured by guns. Every 58 minutes, an African American child dies because of poverty. Every school day, 135,000 African American children bring some kind of weapon to school.

Every day, 100,000 African American children are homeless and some of them are right here in Palm Beach County.

These are overwhelming statistics. A disproportionate share of these young people are African American. What do these statistics tell us? The African-American family is in crisis and has been for a long time. These children live in black neighborhoods surrounded by black churches.

These astounding facts tell us that we have much work to do. We must have a desire to produce profound changes in our families, our neighborhoods, our nation. How can we do this without strong faith? The 21st century has brought challenges for the African American family that can only be solved with mountainous faith and a willingness to step into uncharted territory.

How do we define faith?

Hebrews 1:11 is not merely a definition of faith, but a description of what faith does. There are two key words - 'substance' and 'evidence'. Substance means 'essence' or 'reality'. Faith treats 'things hoped for' as reality. Evidence means 'proof' or 'conviction'. Real faith proves that what is 'unseen' is real, such as our rewards at the return of Christ.

There are volumes of books written about faith. One commentator breaks it down into two parts: (1) *it is the substance of things hoped for*. Faith and hope go together, and the same things that are the object of our hope are the object of our faith. (2) *It is the evidence of things not seen.*

Faith demonstrates to the eye of the mind the reality of those things that cannot be discerned by the eye of the body. The eye of the body can't see it; but the eye of the mind must see it.

The Epistle to the Hebrews was addressed to the Jewish Christians. Christianity was relatively new. New things are not always readily accepted. You can imagine how difficult it was for pioneering Christians. Christianity was radical. It set aside centuries of tradition. It emphasized a new and troubling kind of spiritual freedom. In short, it incurred the wrath of the Jewish religious establishment. The Jewish Christians were criticized, ostracized and demoralized.

Many of them were ready to cut and run and leave the uneasy, uncharted waters of faith for the comfortable, familiar life of works and moral effort. Yes, it takes great courage and faith to be a pioneer in any endeavor.

Women, my questions to you today are: Does your faith foster a pioneering spirit? Will your measure of faith allow you to step into uncharted territory? Will your faith propel you to pursue promises on perilous pathways or swim against the current to greatness, or stand as stalwarts in the storm? Will it?

These are questions that must be asked and answered. We have African-American women who have been educational pioneers, spiritual pioneers, medical pioneers, business and industry pioneers. Rahab is among the people of great faith listed in the faith chapter. But, let's fast forward and step into the pages of history and view three women who had the level of faith that propelled them into uncharted territory. That's what pioneers do. They do what no one has done before. They go where no one has dared go. They forge paths for others to follow. And what they do affect families all over the country.

Constance Baker Motley, a trailblazer in law and politics. She was the first black woman accepted at Columbia Law School, the only woman on the legal team from the Brown vs. Board of Education. She was the first African American to be elected to the New York State Senate, the first African-American to hold the position of Borough President of Manhattan; the first African American woman to serve as a Federal judge. You think she had a measure of faith? Absolutely. She had an impact on the lives of countless Americans. That's what pioneers do. They put their fears away and look at the impact their actions will have on present and future generations. Women of Saint Paul, what is your pioneering spirit leading you to do?

Our second woman is one of great courage.

Mary McLeod Bethune. She started with faith in God, a dream like steel in her soul and $1.50 in her pocket. She built an institution that stands today, educating thousands upon thousands of young people - known as Bethune-Cookman University.

Ms. Bethune, educational pioneer, reminded us that it is faith in God and in ourselves which will protect us. We know her story so well. I don't have to tell you about the odds she was up against. I don't have to tell you about the thousands that told her it couldn't be done, the thousands that prophesied failure. She knew that if she had the kind of faith that Jesus talked about, the faith of a mustard seed, she could move mountains. She understood what James said in the Bible - *faith without works is dead.* She set about matching her faith with works. Her faith moved mountains and the results still stand in Daytona, Fl.

In an excerpt from one of her speeches, she said, "Sometimes as I sit communing in my study I feel that death is not far off....Death neither alarms nor frightens one who has had a long career of fruitful toil....So, as my life draws to a close, I will pass them on to Negroes everywhere in the hope that an old woman's philosophy may give them inspiration.

Here, then is my legacy....I have faith. Faith is the first factor in life devoted to service. Without faith nothing is possible. With it, nothing is impossible. Faith is God's greatest power, but great too, is faith in one's self.....I leave you dignity....I leave you, finally a responsibility to our people....Our children must never lose their zeal for building a better world."

Susie King Taylor was the daughter of slaves born in 1848 during the time when state law prohibited the education of blacks. She went to secret schools taking great risks. By the times she was 14, she was free and was asked by Union authorities to organize a school for the black children. She taught about 40 children and adults in the evening.

Little did the former slave realize that she was an educational pioneer, the first African-American to teach openly in a school for people of color in the state of Georgia. During the Civil War, Taylor married Edward

King, a sergeant in the 33rd U.S. Colored Troops. She traveled with King and his fellow soldiers serving as laundress, nurse and teacher.

With all her good works as an educator, it was in matters of life and death that Susie Taylor made her greatest contribution. Of the more than 5000 women who served in that capacity during the conflict, most were white and middle class and were paid $12.00 for their services. Susie's situation was different. She served almost 3 years and was paid nothing. While the paid nurses stayed at set locations where it was safer, Susie traveled with the regiment. In so doing, she was probably the first woman of color, and the youngest, black or white, to serve as a nurse on the front lines of the Civil War.

When the war was over and they returned to Savannah, Susie's husband died suddenly while she was awaiting the birth of their son. She was alone with no income. She left her son with her mother and took work as a live-in servant with a wealthy white family. Years later, when the family relocated to Boston, she joined them but she had to leave her son.

Tragedy was not finished with Susie; it had one more blow to strike. Her son was seriously ill and she had to go to Shreveport LA to be by her son's bedside. She wanted to take him back with her but no railroad company in the south would sell her a sleeping car berth. Susie said, "*it seemed very hard, when my son's father fought to protect the union and our flag, and yet my son's denied, under this same flag, a berth to carry him home to die, because he was a Negro.*"

In the years following her son's death, and as America

entered the 20th century, Taylor wondered whether the Civil War had been fought in vain. *"All we ask for is equal justice. I hope this day is not far distant when the two races will reside in peace....I know I shall not live to see the day, but it will come."*

Susie King Taylor died in 1912 at the age of 64. I wish I could tell her that today many things have changed. I wish I could tell her about a man named Martin Luther King, Jr. who had the same dream she did. I wish I could her that today, July 2008, we have an African-American male as the Democratic nominee for President of the United States of America. I wish I could tell her, that, yes, there is still much work to be done, but because of the faith of women like her with pioneering spirits who have gone before us, we have marched ahead in this battle for equality and justice. I wish I could tell her that her name lives on in history.

Ladies, each of us can make an impact on the lives of our immediate family and those around us. We may not be a Constance Baker Motley or a Susie King Taylor or a Mary McLeod Bethune. But with faith we can be the best that God has designed us to be. He created us with a purpose. Don't sit on it. You have felt the urging. You've heard that still, quiet voice telling you to go forth. Don't ignore it. Don't use a lack of education, money or youth as an excuse.

Those overwhelming statistics I mentioned at the beginning can only be reduced by exercising the kind of faith that moves mountains. When our young men are being gunned down in the streets, that's a mountain. When our young ladies are more attracted to thugs than decent young men, that's a mountain. When our African-American men are 12% of the general population and more than 40% of the prison population, that's a mountain. Church, it's time for mountain-moving faith.

And men, there's a job for you. Teach our boys how to be real men, how to respect our young women, and teach them that there is no such thing as over-wear. It's called under-wear for a reason.

Older women, teach the younger women how to be respectable young ladies and nurturing mothers. We must do this by example. We can't just talk the talk, we must walk the walk. There's a story of a young mother who was having a talk with her young son as they were preparing dinner together. The mother was telling the boy what Christians should be like and how they should act. When the mother finished explaining the attributes of a Christian, the young boy looked up at her and asked a question: "Mom, have I ever seen a Christian?" The mother was speechless. She had to wonder, what kind of example have I been? We must all ask that same question. What kind of example have we been? What kind of faith do we exhibit?

Without faith, we can only see the physical world around us. Without faith, we are limited by our temporal circumstances and are blind to what God is doing. Without faith, we will never have pioneering spirits. Without faith, we cannot please God.

With faith we can open our spiritual eyes and see the spiritual realities which transcend this world. The world may laugh at us because they see faith as a great waste. They see us giving up the pleasures of this world for something elusive and ethereal. But the world doesn't know what we know.

We know that *faith is the substance of things hoped for; the evidence of things not seen.*

The world is waiting on us to make a difference in our family, our community, our country. The world needs our expertise, our commitment, our diligence, our ability to see a need and fill it, and our pioneering spirits.

Women of God, faith is never easy. But the more convinced we are of the reality of an all-good, all powerful God, the more our trust will grow, and the less we will be overwhelmed by doubts and temptations.

Always include prayer in your daily activities. Get up early in the morning and commune with God. He will direct your paths day by day, hour by hour, minute by minute. Don't be too busy to pray. There is an unknown author who shared this poem:

I got up early one morning and rushed into the day.
I had so much to accomplish that I did not have time to pray.
Problems just tumbled about me, and heavier came each task.
"Why doesn't God help me," I wondered.
He answered, "You didn't ask."
I wanted to see joy and beauty,
But the day toiled on, gray and bleak;
I wondered why God did not show me,
He said, "But you did not seek."
I tried to come into God's presence;
I used all my keys at the lock.
God gently and lovingly chided,
"My child, you did not knock."
I woke up early this morning,
and paused before entering the day;
I had so much to accomplish
that I had to take time to pray.

Sisters, when you leave here today, leave knowing what you are going to do to impact your family, your church, your community. Know that you have talent, the skill, the potential to do great things. Know that with faith you, too, can forge new pathways and go where no one has dared go or do what no one has dared to do.

Know that your Creator instilled greatness in you while you were yet in your mother's womb. Know that faith is the key. But most of all, know that we cannot look at faith without seeing the cross, Because the more we can trust in the absolute truth of the resurrection of our Lord and Savior, Jesus Christ, the more we will demonstrate pioneering spirits.

RIGHTEOUS
RELATIONSHIPS

And grieve not the Holy Spirit of God, whereby you are
sealed unto the day of redemption. Let all bitterness, and
wrath, and anger, and clamor, and evil speaking, be put
away from you. With all malice: And be ye kind one to
another, tenderhearted, forgiving one another, even as
God for Christ's sake hath forgiven you.
Ephesians 4:30-32

Ephesians is one of the four prison epistles of Paul that
was written while he was imprisoned in Rome. Ephesians
tells us that the church is a living organism, the actual body
of Christ. This Epistle is about unity in the body of Christ.
It helps us to understand our personal relationships with
Jesus. It teaches us how to live with our fellow Christians

in a nurturing, mature relationship.

In the early days, the gospel was not just spoken, it walked in shoe leather; it worked. What we see here in Ephesians is the church revealed as God's masterpiece. I am sure Solomon's Temple was magnificent, but no man-made temple, not even Solomon can compare with God's church. God's church is constructed of living stones, indwelt by the Holy Spirit. There is no reason for me or you to think we are the whole church and nothing can happen or go forth without us. We are just one stone that makes up the invisible building.

We, the believers, are in this world to walk as Christ walked, serve as Christ served, and love as Christ loved. Because one of these days, the church will leave this world and be presented to Christ as a bride. Oh, what a wonderful, beautiful, glorious day that is going to be.

We learn in verse 30 that we should not grieve or cause sorrow to the Holy Spirit. We do this whenever we do little ugly things like use unholy speech or think dirty thoughts or lie on one another. When any person is grieved, it breaks fellowship. We don't want to do that.

The last thing in the world we want to do is provoke the blessed spirit of God to withdraw his presence from us. If God takes His Holy Spirit away from us, we will find ourselves engaged in a losing struggle with sin. We will sound like Paul in the 7th chapter of Romans: "I do not understand what I do, for what I want to do, I do not do, but what I hate, I do... what a wretched man I am." If God takes His Holy Spirit away, that old Adamic nature will completely take over.

Verse 31 tells us about some stumbling blocks, some roadblocks that will get in the way of developing righteous relationships with Jesus Christ and each other. Paul says we must put these things away.

Paul starts out with the term "bitterness. Bitterness is characterized by a showing of intense hostility: resentful or cynical. Nothing pleases a bitter person and she complains about everything. When we speak out of bitterness to other people, it hurts and this grieves the Holy Spirit. Bitterness leads to wrath and wrath produces anger and anger provokes clamour and evil speaking.

Malice takes in all of the others that have been mentioned. It is deep-seated, rooted anger that prompts men to plot all kinds of evil against his fellow man. It's a desire to inflict harm or suffering on another.

It is congealed hatred. Of all the things Paul says we must put away, he mentions bitterness first. That's because bitterness leads to all the others.

Hebrews 12:15 says *"Look after each other so that not one of you will fail to find God's best blessings. Watch out that no bitterness take root among you, for as it springs up it causes deep trouble, hurting many in their spiritual lives."*

A lot of the anger in our communities has come from a root of bitterness that began during slavery and was passed down from generation to generation. Most of Satan's schemes against African Americans were rooted in the experience of slavery. As we look back through the annals of history, we are reminded that we were severely mistreated. The women were raped. The men were beaten.

The children were separated from parents. We were used and abused. Out of all of the frustration and helplessness we experienced, bitterness found root in the souls of our ancestors.

That bitterness has been passed down from parents to children because there was no other place to vent frustration. They couldn't vent to their masters. Years later, they couldn't bent to their bosses. Even when slavery was over, parents still had to deal with rejection and frustration from society.

Even now, when we are wronged by those over us, we will sometimes take it out on the people that are under our control. Your boss makes you mad at work and you come home and kick the cat or yell at your children. I had some very stressful days when I worked in corporate America. My older daughter, Lisa, could tell when I'd had an especially bad day at work. She would watch me as I got out of the car in the evening and based on the expression on my face, she would say to the younger daughter, "Tosha, don't get on mama's nerves today".

Bitterness must be recognized, repented of, and healed through the grace of God. We can't keep looking back and saying we are bitter because....We have to be healed of this bitterness through the grace of God.

One seed of bitterness can ruin an entire congregation. The church of Ephesus is being told by Paul to put these negative things away. They tamper with or destroy the unity of the church.

We must put away the old man and put on the new man.

Verse 32 says, "*And be kind one to another, tender hearted, forgiving one another, even as God for Christ's sake hath forgiven you.*"

First of all we are to be kind to one another. We can be mean to each other sometimes. A kind person has a benevolent nature or disposition. A kind person is mild and gentle. And don't mistake kindness for weakness; it is simply Christian courtesy. On a talk show, it was discussed that middle school girls 12-14 years, traveled in packs, bullied other girls, and picked on them until they cried. Where did they learn this meanness? Whose behavior are they emulating? Who are their role models? Have they learned this from us? It doesn't hurt to be kind to each other. Kindness is a language which the deaf can hear and the blind can see.

Paul talks about tender-heartedness. That's soft-hearted; empathy and sympathy. A kind-hearted person is quickly moved to compassion for another. "I feel you" as the young people say.

And finally, forgiving one another. This is not a command under the law but it is on the basis of the grace of God. We should forgive, not because it is the law, but because we have been forgiven over and over again.

In the sermon On the Mount, Christ stated the legal grounds for forgiveness when He said "*For if ye forgive men their trespasses, your heavenly Father will also forgive you, but if ye forgive not men their trespasses, neither will your Father forgive your trespasses*" Matt 6:14-15. But here in Ephesians we are told to forgive on the basis of the grace of God. What a blessing!

In the 18th chapter of Matthew, we find the servant who was forgiven a huge debt. But he went out and grabbed a man who owed him a teensy-weensy debt, choked him, threw him into jail. He was owed just a fraction of what he was forgiven, and yet, he wouldn't forgive. How soon we forget.

There has to be a give and take relationship when it comes to the faults of one another. Rather than making a big-to-do over the faults of others, we are to forgive. It's not easy, I know what it takes.

It takes divine love (agape) to live graciously in the world, and to hold the right attitude towards others. Paul is speaking of relationships within the Christian community, not out in the world. Love and forgiveness must prevail in the household of faith if men apart from our Lord are to see the possibilities of grace from themselves.

Question: What can we do to make sure that righteousness finds expression in human relationships?

1. Put off falsehood and speak the truth. This involves more than not lying. It involves an open sharing of ourselves with each other.

2. Do not let anger dictate our actions. Don't give it a place. Move towards reconciliation before the sun goes down.

3. Reject gossip of any kind. Seek to build others up, not tear them down.

EXAMPLE: "Hi Mary, Listen, girl. We have some praying to do. Sister Annie's husband left her for that young woman down the street. You know the one who wears those skimpy short dresses. She's been goin' with him for a long time. I heard the mortgage payment is two months behind. I haven't seen that fancy car lately, you? I believe it's been repossessed. Yeah, we gotta pray. It's so sad...OOPS, that's my other line. See you later.

Did they pray? No. What have they just done? They have wrapped gossip in a thinly disguised request for prayer. Their motive was not sincere. She didn't call her to seek prayer. Her intention all along was to spread gossip. Personal lives, marriages, ministries have been ruined by malicious gossip. Sometimes the gossip was nothing than rumors. But even if it's true, we do not have the right to spread it. Check yourself the next time you are tempted to talk about something that may or may not be true and furthermore, is not your business. One reason the dog has so many friends, he wags his tail instead of his tongue.

> 4. Get rid of bitterness, rage, slander and every form of malice. In their place, we need to show kindness and compassion, forgiving each other as God has forgiven us.

Another question: How can we build a healthy church full of righteous relationships?"

> 1. See leaders as equippers. Their purpose is to help equip us to serve better in this Christian community. We have to accept them as leaders and respect them. Remember, they are called, not us.

> 2. See each member as a minister. My pastor always says, "We are not always preachers, but we

are all ministers."

3. Get to know each other well. If you always sit on the same side of the sanctuary, introduce yourself to someone on the other side. It's hard to love a person you have not personally met.

4. Learn to share our lives with each other. Love involves bearing each other's burdens. We need to trust others enough to reveal our burdens to them. If my sister is carrying a heavy burden, she can lean on my shoulder. Tomorrow, it may be my time to lean on her shoulder.

It is sad when you have a church where people have not come together as one. There are older women, middle aged women, younger women. We all should be able to relate to each other.

Our young girls need to be pulled into this fold, into the relationship of the family. Sometimes, women, our young girls feel so left out. Sometimes, they have problems they will not express, because they have been burned. They have come to us, seasoned women of God, and poured out their hearts and then heard everything they said in the streets and all over the community. So, when they have problems, they don't come back to us. We have to be careful about that.

Sisters, when we counsel our younger women and young girls, let's do it in non-condemnatory tones. Let's keep it confidential and avoid spreading hurt. Let us be involved in righteous relationships with each other regardless of age. Everybody is not where you are spiritually. You've had a long walk with Christ. Someone else's walk with Christ has been shorter, or just starting.

No, they haven't reached perfection yet, and neither have we. We are all still under construction, just at different stages of completion. Don't judge. Don't condemn. Don't accuse. Let's just wrap each other in love. When we come together in love, the enemy cannot break our bond.

Relationships within the church should be marked by love. Jesus said at the last supper - *"love ye one another as I have loved you."* He loved us so much that He walked up Golgotha's hill carrying my sins and your sins on his shoulders. He died a slow, humiliating, excruciating death because He loved us. While He was dying, He prayed, *"Father, forgive them"*. Church, we don't have the right not to forgive.

Jesus Christ, my savior, born in a strangers barn and buried in a borrowed tomb, got up early Sunday morning with all power in His hands. That's my Savior. Is He your Savior? I thank God for a Savior that taught us how to love and forgive because love and forgiveness is the only way we can have righteous relationships.

THE COST OF CHRISTMAS

Everything has a price. We are in the season that emphasizes giving. God gave so much when He gave us Jesus. A gift is free to the receiver, but it cost the giver. The birth of Jesus was a gift to humanity, for John 3:16 says *"For God so loved the world that He gave His only begotton Son, that whosoever believes in Him shall not perish, but shall have everlasting life."* This precious gift did not cost us anything, but it cost God everything. How dare we treat it lightly. Other than God, did it cost anybody else?

Let's think about that.

1. What did it cost Joseph? History says very little about Joseph. He is barely a footnote on the pages of time, but Joseph was a man, a real man. Joseph was not aware of the holy conception, so when he learned that Mary was pregnant, he was hurt. He decided to divorce her quietly, because he was a just man. He did not want to humiliate her publicly. It cost him his pride. The woman to whom he was betrothed had betrayed him or so he thought.

Betrothal then was more binding than the engagements of today. This bethrothal had cost Joseph at least part of the bride's cost. There was something called bridewealth that the groom had to pay to the bride's father somewhere between 10 and 50 shekels. You didn't get a bride for nothing in those days. His money is spent, his pride is hurt and his ego is wounded. It's going to take an angel to clear this situation up. When the angel spoke to Joseph, he swallowed his pride and listened to the angel.

How would men react today when told, "This is not your baby. It's conceived by the Holy Spirit."

Can you imagine the reaction? "What do you mean, you haven't been with anybody, yet you expecting. What kind of fool you think I am?" For these men today, it would take more than one angel, it would take a legion of angels. But Joseph was satisfied with the angel's explanation. Thank God for angels that God can use to turn any situation around.

2. What did it cost the wise men? Just before the death of Herod, the wise men arrived in Judea searching for the newborn king of the Jews. Herod instructed them to report to him the whereabouts of the child as soon as they found him. The visit of the wise men reveals the true identity of the infant as the long-expected and prophesied royal Messiah of Israel. Their cost was only money, but a lot of money.

One said, *Gold have I to crown Him a king.* Gold

represents the fact that He was born a king. Gold was not cheap, a most appropriate gift for a king.

Another said, *Frankincense to offer have I*. Incense speaks of the fragrance of his life and his deity. It was costly because it came from a tree that only grew in Sheba in Southern Arabia. The costly value and its use for worship made the presentation of frankincense to the infant Jesus an appropriate gift.

Another said, *Myrrh is mine, its bitter perfume breathes a life of gathering gloom*. Myrrh was held in high regard as a perfume and also as an embalming oil. Myrrh speaks of his death. This gift will be left out at His second coming. The next time He comes, He won't come to die. He will come as King of Kings and Lord of Lords.

Even as the wise men honored the baby, Jesus, Herod and possibly the chief priests and scribes of the people plotted the baby's death. Herod, a brutal man who executed his own sons and wife, was already under a death sentence from an incurable disease. But he wanted to make sure no Jewish messiah took the throne from his descendants.

After the wise men presented their gifts, they were warned not to return by the same route. They returned via a different route. After we meet Jesus, we too, have to go a different way. Joseph was warned to flee Egypt because of Herod's intention to kill Jesus. Joseph took his family and left Bethlehem.

3. What did it cost the town of Bethlehem?
O, little town of Bethlehem,

How still we see thee lie!
Above thy deep and dreamless sleep
The silent stars go by.

Bethlehem was the birthplace of Jesus. It was also the home of Boaz, Ruth, Obed, Jesse and David. It was just a village with wheat fields that later gave way to barley. Bethlehem was associated with the Patriarchs. Rachel died and was buried in its vicinity. It's a place where cultivated fields still occupy patches between the many ravines.

Was there a cost for Bethlehem? Yes, they paid dearly. Allow me to use my imagination to tell you a story that illustrates the cost of Christmas to this little town of Bethlehem.

Asher and his wife, Sherah lived simple lives. They had their little farm with wheat and some animals. Times weren't easy, but with hard work they were able to survive. In the evenings, they would sit around the fire and enjoy each other's company.

This year they had something to be especially happy about. Sherah had given birth to their first child - a son.

One evening after a long day, Asher and his wife Sherah sat in front of the fire warming themselves and admiring their first born son, Jemah. He was a fine healthy baby. Asher had great plans for his son. He was growing big and strong and he was now six-months old.

As Asher and Sherah discussed their future plans for their lives, they heard a great noise. Before Asher could rise to look outside, the door burst open and armed solders strode boldly in.

They snatched the baby out of Sherah's arms and after checking the sex of the baby and finding it to be a male, in one swift move the baby was killed and left bleeding on the floor. Sherah screamed, "My baby, Oh God of Abraham, my baby." Asher was screaming," not my son, not my son."

Asher could do nothing to protect his child, because he was grossly outnumbered. The pain he felt and saw in his wife's eyes was almost unbearable. As they hugged each other they could hear screams all over the hillsides. Other families were suffering the same loss. All because one man, Herod, was afraid of losing his throne to a little baby boy.

The families with male children two and under paid a high price for the first Christmas. It cost them the life of their sons. But Bethlehem had to go on.

> *Yet in thy dark streets shineth, The everlasting Light,*
> *The hopes and fears of all the years, Are met in thee tonight.*

4. **What does it cost us?** It doesn't cost us our pride. It doesn't cost us gold, frankincense or myrrh. It doesn't cost us the lives of our sons. All we have to do is love the Lord with all our hearts and all our souls and our neighbors as ourselves. Christmas is all about love. The love that's spoken of in John 3:16 comes with a duty, an obligation "to believe in Jesus Christ." And if we believe, there's a benefit; we shall not perish, but have everlasting life.

Jesus Christ was born to die for us, to bear our sins.

We should never relegate Christmas to the annals of history. After the cost that has been paid, we should fight to keep Christ in Christmas. I think of this when I hear: Happy Holidays, Seasons Greetings. What happened to "Merry Christmas?" I think of this when I am tempted to abbreviate Christmas by writing "xmas". The "X" can not replace Christ. Christmas should always be the most important and sacred time of the year.

" For unto us a child is born, unto us a son is given and the government shall be upon his shoulders, and His name shall be called Wonderful, Counselor, the Mighty God, the Everlasting Father, the Prince of Peace. "

A BLUEPRINT FOR PRAYER

And it came to pass, that, as he was praying in a certain place, when he ceased, one of his disciples said unto him, Lord teach us to pray, as John also taught his disciples.
Luke 11:1

When one wants to know how to effectively accomplish a specialized task, an expert is consulted.

If you want to know how to play a decent game of golf, ask Tiger Woods. If you want a great lesson in tennis, ask the Williams sisters. If you want to know how to build a bridge, ask a civil engineer; if you want to know how to restore an antique car, ask my husband. If you want to know how to bake a lemon pound cake, ask my mother.

The disciples wanted to know how to pray. Jesus is the One to ask. As believers, we are builders in the kingdom. Whether we are building a tool shed, a house, a mall or the Crowne Plaza Hotel, we need a plan - a blueprint.

The topic today is "A Blueprint for Prayer." *"The effectual fervent prayer of a righteous man availeth much."* We need to know how to pray effectively. So we're going to go to the Master for a magnificent blueprint.

The disciples followed Jesus faithfully. They heard Him preach masterful sermons - sermons that stirred the very hearts of men, sermons that fed spiritually hungry souls, sermons that have never been and will never be equaled. But they didn't say, "Master, teach us how to preach."

The disciples walked with Jesus day in and day out. They saw Him heal a blind man in a crowded noisy street. They saw Him heal the lepers when no one else would go near them. They saw Him heal a woman who had suffered twelve long years, but they didn't say, "Master, teach us how to heal."

They saw Jesus minister to tormented souls. They saw Him cast out demons. But they didn't say, "Master teach us how to cast out demons." Instead they said, "Master, teach us to pray." They were not just asking how to pray. The Lord had given the Sermon on the mount which outlined how to pray.

The disciples were not asking for a technique, a system, an art form or a ritual to follow. It was not a matter of how to do it, but they wanted to pray like Christ prayed.

Prayer was central to the ministry of Jesus and He wanted it to be a vital part of their ministry. So when the disciples asked, Jesus responded. That's what I like about Jesus. When we ask, He responds. He gave them what's commonly called "The Lord's Prayer." That's the model prayer. Although it's called the Lord's prayer, that's really a misnomer because there's a passage in there that says *forgive us our sins*. Jesus didn't sin, so this prayer is not for Him, but for the disciples and us.

This little prayer serves as a blueprint for us. It has eight power points: God's Paternity, God's Person, God's Program, God's Purpose, God's Provision, God's Pardon, God's Protection, and God's Preeminence.

1. God's Paternity - "OUR FATHER"
Jesus taught us who to pray to - not saints or angels - but to God the Father. Jesus alone guarantees that we can enter into a relationship with God and become members of his family. He is our Father and we are His children. John 1:12 states: *"But as many as received Him, to them He gave the right to become children of God, even to those who believe in His name."* That's the doctrine of adoption. The privilege of adoption is entirely due to faith in Christ. He became the Son of man, that the sons and daughters of men might become the sons and daughters of God Almighty.

2. God's Person - "HALLOWED BE THY NAME"
In Psalm 9:10 we read, *"And those who know your name will put their trust in You."* What the psalmist was saying here is that those of us who know God's character and God's power will put our trust in Him. In prayer, we must seek first the kingdom of God and the righteousness thereof, by ascribing honor to His holy name, and power to his government.

So when we pray *"hallowed be thy name"*, we are praying that God will be God to us, that He will be set apart in our prayers in such a way that it will be clear that we reverence God.

3. God's Program: "THY KINGDOM COME"
Rev. 11:15b states *."..The kingdom of the world has become the kingdom of our Lord and of his Christ, and he will reign forever and ever."* When we pray *"Thy kingdom Come"*, we look to that joyous time when God's Messianic Kingdom

prophesied throughout the Old Testament will be established when Jesus returns to earth. We ask that on this small bit of earth we occupy now, we will submit our will to God's will. When we pray *"Thy Kingdom come"* we acknowledge God's right to rule over all people, including us.

4. God's Purpose: "THY WILL BE DONE"
Praying for His will to be done provides a foundation for our prayers. For us to live according to God's will *"on earth as it is done in heaven"* is to do so in enemy territory. To live in a realm that is controlled by Satan is to recognize that this present world is an enemy to God. For us to do God's will *"on earth as it is in Heaven"*, sometimes it may be hard. We may have to swim against the current. When the world is going left, we have to go right. When we pray, *"Thy will be done on earth as it is in Heaven"*, We are praying for our friends, our families, our society, but above all for ourselves. We have to stay in God's will just as Jesus had to stay in His Father's will.

And it wasn't easy at the end for Jesus to stay in His Father's will for we hear Him praying in **Matt. 26:39**. *"O my Father, if it be possible, let this cup pass from me: nevertheless not as I will, but as You will."* And the 42nd verse: *"He went away again the second time, and prayed saying, O my Father, if this cup may not pass away from Me, except I drink it, Your will be done.*

5. God's Provision: "GIVE US OUR DAILY BREAD"
When Jesus said, "Give us today our daily bread," He was making a point that it is OK and all right to pray for our daily needs. At the end, I will come back with an illustration of this power point.

6. God's Pardon: "FORGIVE US OUR SINS"
After we ask the Father for provision, we ask for pardon, *"Forgive us our sins."* Notice that "forgive" follows "give." Jesus is so awesome. He very smartly linked the two

petitions - give us our daily bread with forgive us our sins. He linked them so that when we think of our need for food, we will recognize our need for pardon, too. We are encouraged every day to come to the throne of Grace and plead for mercy.

To sin is human, to forgive divine. We are never closer to God's grace than when we admit our sin and cry out for pardon. "Lord, I've sinned against you. I am so sorry. Please, Lord, forgive me for my sins."

7. God's Protection: "LEAD US NOT INTO TEMPTATION'

Behind the temptation stands the tempter, behind the lies stands the liar - Satan himself. When we pray "*lead us not into temptation*", we are crying out - "Lord, please keep me away from temptation. Don't let me fall into Satan's trap. The Lord's Prayer reminds us to beware of the strategies of Satan because he is here for one reason - to conquer our souls. When we pray "*deliver us from the evil one*", we recognize Satan's power, we affirm our own weakness, and plead to the greater power of God.

8. God's Preeminence: "THE KINGDOM, POWER, AND THE GLORY"

This is the doxology that ends the prayer. These last lines are an affirmation of praise. Rev. 5:13 states: "*And every creature which is in heaven, and on the earth and under the earth, and such as are in the sea, and all that are in them, heard I saying, Blessing and Honor and Glory, and Power, be to Him that sets upon the throne and to the Lamb forever and ever.*" When we pray as we should, we affirm God's majesty, we trumpet His power, and through the answers to our prayers, we display His glory.

Now, let us re-visit Power Point #5. GOD'S PROVISIONS - "GIVE US OUR DAILY BREAD."

This story was shared in "Think and Grow Rich" by Napoleon Hill. I have used my imagination to determine what brought on this incident.

Mr. Darby owned an old-fashioned wheat grinding mill and he operated a large farm. On this farm were a number of "colored" share-croppers. During this time, back in the thirties, they didn't call us African-Americans or Black or Negro, we were "colored".

So one day Mr. Darby was very busy and the door opened and a little colored girl whose family was one of the share-cropping tenants came in and took her place by the door. Mr. Darby, who was very mean with a terrible temper, looked up and saw the little colored girl and he yelled at her: "What do you want?" He wasn't very kind. Very meekly, she said, "My mama say send her fifty cents."

"I won't do it, now get out of here and go home." "Yassuh", she said. She had manners. She said "yassuh", but she didn't move. Now when she said "yassuh", Mr. Darby went on about his work thinking she was going to run on home, but she stood right there by the door. When he looked up again, she was still standing there.

And he said, 'Didn't I tell you to go home?" And she said, "Yassuh", but she didn't move. Her defiance made him angry, and he dropped the sack of grain he was getting ready to pour into the mill hopper and he picked up a barrel stave. That's something like a stick with a sharp point on the end.

And he started towards that little girl and he had an expression on his face that said there's goin' to be trouble in this camp. Now Mr. Darby's nephew was also present and he was very concerned for the little girl because he knew his uncle had a terrible temper; he was scared for her but too scared to say anything. So he held his breath.

Mr. Darby got closer and closer to the little girl with that stick in his hand. She didn't move an inch. He got almost up on her. At that point I would have been getting up out of there, but the little colored girl took a step forward and said, "**My mama's got to have that fifty cents**."

He was shocked. He stepped back and he looked at her. Now remember, this was in the thirties and this was a little colored girl talking to a white man like that. He stepped back, reached in his pocket and pulled out that fifty cents. And he gave it to that little girl.

She took that money, slowly backed out of that door and never took her eyes off him. And when she had gone, Mr. Darby sat down on a box and looked out the window staring into space for ten minutes. He had just been conquered by a little colored girl. He couldn't understand what happened.

Why did he give in to this little girl? How was she able to master him? He and his nephew discussed it. What happened here? What just happened here? It had never happened before.

No "colored" person would dare defy a white man, especially one providing his bread and butter. But you see, what they didn't know, Mr. Darby was the answer to someone's prayer. He wasn't in control here. A Higher Power was at work. Sometimes, we are the vehicle God uses to answer another person's prayer.

I imagine this is what led to the confrontation between Mr. Darby and the little colored girl. Early that morning, the little girl's mother, a share-cropper, got up. Share-cropping was a hard life. I've heard the stories and I'm sure you've heard them too about how our ancestors worked the whole year and at the end of the year when they tallied up with the owner, instead of getting paid, they ended up owing money.

And so it was a hard life. I've heard my parents talk about it. They traveled the circuits for a while working the farms out west of Palm Beach and Broward County. As a matter of fact, I was born in a row house on the edge of a bean field on the range-line. So I can imagine this little colored girl's mother that morning.

She looked in the meal barrel, and there was no meal. She looked in the flour barrel, and there was no flour. She looked in the pantry and the shelves were empty. Then she looked into the eyes of her children and she saw hunger. And she cried out. "Our Father, which art in heaven, Hallowed be Thy name, Thy kingdom come, Thy will be done. My Father, my God, my children are hungry, and I have not a penny, not a drop of flour, not a drop of meal. But Lord, I know that you will give us this day our daily bread. Lord, I'm asking for an answer. My children are hungry, Lord, so give us this day our daily bread."

And the mother of the little colored girl prayed from the depths of her soul. And the answer came. The Holy Spirit whispered, "Send a child to Mr. Darby for fifty cents." And the Devil said, "You think the man that's cheating you out of your crop money is going to give you fifty cents, that's impossible." But the Holy Spirit whispered, "THERE ARE NO IMPOSSIBILITIES WITH GOD." You gotta know which voice to listen to. Now, you could do a lot with fifty cents in those days. With fifty cents you could buy flour and sugar and meal.

And so the mother called one of her little girls and told her, "You go and ask Mr. Darby for fifty cents. And stay there until he gives it to you." The little girl knew how important that fifty cents was to her mother. She knew it meant the difference in whether or not her sisters and brothers ate or went to bed hungry again.

When Mr. Darby told her "no" and told her to go home, it didn't matter to her . She stayed there. It didn't matter if he took out a stick to her. She stayed there. Even if he had whipped her, it wouldn't have mattered. All that mattered was that he gave her that fifty cents.

We must learn like the little girl that when we pray, we must stand firm and wait on Him, for the answer will come. Don't move. Stay there. Don't let circumstances move you. Stay there. Don't let winds of adversity move you. Stay there. Stand on His word that says *"I have never seen the righteous forsaken nor His seed begging bread."*

I thank God for Jesus. Do you thank God for Jesus? I thank God that when we pray to our Father, Jesus is even at the right hand of God making intercession for us.

Wonderful Savior. Precious Savior. We thank you for the blueprint for prayer.

Thank you and may God bless you abundantly.

THE CHRISTIAN RACE

Wherefore seeing we also are compassed about with so great a cloud of witnesses, let us lay aside every weight, and the sin which doth so easily beset us, and let us run with patience the race that is set before us. Looking unto Jesus the author and finisher of our faith:........

Hebrew 12:1, 2a

This Christian life is a race. It is a long distance race. It's not a sprint or a 100 yard dash. It's a long, long race. In this race, we only go around one time and this is not a practice run. This passage of Scripture is telling us that everybody has a race to run. It does no good to stand on the side lines and watch someone else run the race. The Christian race is not a spectator sport. We all must get in the race and the goal is the same for everybody. The finish line is Salvation.

There is a danger in standing still. This Word is telling us that we have to move out for God. If we get caught out in a snow storm, we couldn't stand still or we would freeze to death. The first step in that process is falling asleep. So we would have to keep moving. As sure as we fall asleep, we will surely die.

In a spiritual sense we have to keep moving or we will stagnate and eventually die. We must move forward in our relationship with Christ so that we can come to know him intimately. We need to cultivate this relationship because there is joy in knowing him.

Verse one starts out with the word, *wherefore*. This word cements the chapter that goes before with the chapter that is coming up. *"Wherefore seeing we also are compassed about with so great a cloud of witnesses."* Compassed means surrounding. There are witnesses everywhere. These witnesses were acknowledged in the previous chapter. The string of witnesses are the testifiers.

The witnesses are the ones who have already run the race down here. And they ran it by faith. Those witnesses whom the world consider great successes ran the race by faith. Rahab had faith that if she helped the spies escape, she and her family would be saved. The eleventh chapter of Hebrews acknowledges men of great faith. Some of the witnesses suffered and were slain by the sword, some of them died terrible deaths, especially the disciples. They all died martyrs. Their testimonies of faith encourage us to run by faith and live by faith. The heroes of the past were not spectators, but inspiring examples.

The Word says, *Let us run with patience the race that is set before us.* We have to get out of the grandstand; get off the pews; go down on the racetrack of life. We've got to do whatever God has called us to do; however He has called us to do it; wherever He has called us to do it. Did He call you to be a missionary? Did He call you to be a teacher? Did He call you to be a friend to the friendless? The whole thought in this Scripture is that we have to move out for God.

We have people who come to church every Sunday. They are spectators. They're not really on the racetrack. But in the Christian race, we can't afford to be spectators. We can't make it to the finish line as a spectator. We know the finish line is Salvation.

Races can be won or lost. But the Christian race is the only race where everybody can win. It doesn't matter if you don't have great speed. The race isn't given to the swift. Paul wrote in Corinthians, *"Know ye not that they which in a race run all, but one receives the prize."* In an athletic event, only one person can claim first prize. But in this Christian race, all of can win a prize if we are obeying the Word of God. Paul went on the say, *I therefore so run, not as uncertainly....."* (I Cor 9:24, 26). Paul was not playing at this thing. This race is real.

This first verse gives us a duty which consists of two parts: Preparatory and Perfective.

1. Preparatory: Notice as athletes prepare to run their race, they strip off warm-up jackets, jogging pants and any unnecessary clothing. They travel light. Paul said, *"Lay aside every weight, and the sin that doth so easily beset us. Weight*s are concern for the body and the things of the world that distract us from our Christian walk. *Sin that so easily beset us* is the sin that has the greatest advantage over us - the sin that holds us back. Each of us must determine what that is and remove it from our life. In preparing for this race, it is absolutely imperative that we get rid of excess baggage. Running with weights is like running with a load of bricks on our back and cement shoes. You'll never make it to the finish line.

Please be aware that hatred carries a weight. If you are envious, that's a weight. Unbelief is as heavy as a fifty pound sack of potatoes. Lack of trust weighs a ton. Don't mention unforgiveness - that will double you over with weight. Any of these extra weights will make your race hard to run. We have to be light-footed to run this race.

Once we have laid aside the weights and sins that hold us back, we go into the perfective stage.

2. Perfective: *"Run with patience the race that is set before us."* This race is already marked out before us by the Word of God and the examples of the faithful servants of God - that cloud of witnessed that are talked about in Hebrews 11: Abraham, Isaac, Jacob, Moses, Joseph. And that's not all of them. That's just some of them. This race must be run with patience and perseverance. We can't be like some of the early Hebrews who tempted to quit because of persecution. There are going to be obstacles, but faith and patience are the conquering grace.

Verse two says, *"Looking unto Jesus the author and finisher of our faith."*

We mentioned great witnesses who are inspiring examples to us. But we have a greater example than any of these mentioned before - Our Lord and Savior Jesus Christ. He is not only the object of our faith, but the author. He is the finisher of grace, and of the work of faith with power in the souls of his people; And he is the judge and rewarder of our faith. Our faith has beginning in Him and is completed in Him. He is both the start and the end of the race. He is also the supreme witness who has already run the race and overcome.

We can look to Him **in** everything, **for** everything, **with** everything and **through** everything.

We must look to Jesus in everything, *"for in him we live, and move, and have our being."* Many of us are ready to look to Jesus when trouble is on our heels. We run to him, we cry out to Him. But when everything is going well, we lean on our own finite strength and we fail. We fail miserably. Look to Jesus in everything - in good times and bad times, in joy and in sorrow, in lean times and bountiful times, in triumph as well as trial. The Scripture admonishes us to look to Jesus *"that we may obtain mercy, and find grace to help in time of need"* (Heb 4:16)

Look to Jesus *for* everything. *"And whatsoever ye shall ask in my name, that will I do"* (John 14:13) Some of us don't depend on the Lord to supply all our needs. We rely on self-effort and other people. We set ourselves up for disappointment. We should look to Jesus for life, love, food, clothing, and shelter - everything. The Word says whatsoever we ask, not just certain things, but whatsoever. We are promised ample supply for all our needs, *"according to his riches in glory by Christ Jesus"* (Phil 4:19)

Look to Jesus **with** everything. *"And I pray God your whole spirit and soul and body be preserved blameless."* (I Thess. 5:23) Some Christians fail to totally look to Jesus. They reserve a portion of their life for self. If we're to be victorious, we must look to Jesus with everything - time, talent, and treasure. We must be totally dedicated to Him. Paul urged us to *"present our bodies a living sacrifice, holy, acceptable unto God"* (Rom. 12:1). Now, that's total dedication.

Look to Jesus *through* everything. *"After that ye have suffered a while....establish, strengthen, settle you"* (I Peter 5:10). Through your triumphs and your trials, look to Jesus. It's easy to look to Jesus through our happy times, but let us not complain and blame God when suffering strikes. God often allows suffering to strengthen our faith and fulfill his purpose. We must continue to look to Jesus and seek his purpose with patience and trust. When we are traveling through valley experiences, Peter advised us to, *"Rejoice, inasmuch as ye are partakers of Christ's sufferings"* (I Peter 4:13).

So, saints, while we are running this Christian race with patience and perseverance, let us look to Jesus, the author and finisher of our faith, for everything.

Excuses vs. Commitment

And they with one consent began to make excuse. The first said unto him, I have bought a piece ground, and I must needs to go and see it: I pray thee have me excused, And another said, I have bought five yoke of oxen, and I go to prove them: I pray thee have me excused. And another said, I have married a wife, and therefore I cannot come.

Luke 14: 18-20

Just prior to this passage, Jesus had gone out to dinner, a very nice dinner, at the home of one of the Pharisees. Luke is the only one who records this incident. Jesus taught the host and the other guests some manners after healing a man with the dropsy. He looked the guests straight in their eyes and corrected their manners. Then he corrected the host; it created a little tension. That brings us to verse 15.

One of the guests made an attempt to ease the tension by throwing out a cliche: *"Blessed is he that shall eat bread in the kingdom of God."* I don't know what he meant by that, and he probably didn't either, but Jesus didn't let him get away with it. He said to him, *"A certain man made a great supper , and invited many: And sent his servant at supper time to say to them that were invited, Come, for all things are ready."*

It was the custom to send the invitations out early, but as time drew nearer for the dinner, a personal invitation was extended.

God issued an invitation for salvation. What are we going to do with it? Are we going to accept? Or are we going to make excuses as to why we can't accept? There is no feast greater than salvation; we can't buy our way into it. We can't crash that party. We can only come by the grace of God. Ephesians 2:8,9 tell us that *"For grace are ye saved by faith: and that not of yourselves: it is the gift of God: not of works, lest any man should boast."*

The way we get into this dinner is by receiving a gift. The only thing that will exclude us from heaven is a refusal to accept the invitation.

Jesus wants them to know what men are doing with God's invitation. What kind of excuses are being used? There are three kinds of excuses used here:

        1. Possessions
        2. Business
        3. Natural Affection

Verse 18: Possessions. This man said he had to go see a piece of land that he had already bought. Is this an excuse or an alibi? Or an outright lie? Someone said: "An alibi is a lie stuffed in the skin of an excuse." This man was either a liar or a fool. Would you buy a piece of property without seeing it first? I wouldn't. It could be land in the swamps of Florida.

Verse 19: Business. This man had to test his oxen. He should have tested them before he bought them. Don't you always test drive a car before you buy it? He is like the first man- either a liar or a fool. Couldn't they come up with some excuses that were a little more original or believable? First, how are you going to plow at night? At night it was probably as dark then as our city was when all the lights went out during the hurricanes.

Also, a man with five yoke of oxen would be wealthy enough to have someone working for him. This excuse does not hold water.

People get so busy with business they have no time for God. They spend every waking moment climbing the corporate ladder. Sunday is a day used to conduct more business or rest up from those eighty hour weeks so they can start the rat race all over again Monday morning. And when we are dead and done from the stress of the business, the business goes on without us.

Verse 20: Natural Affection. The first two excuses were bad enough. But this excuse is really weak. I know he could have thought of something better. Why didn't he bring his wife to dinner with him? There was a law in Israel that excused a man from going to war if he had taken a new wife, but there was no law that excused him from going to dinner.

Verses 21-24 tell us that the master sent his servant to bring in the poor, maimed and the blind. And yet there was room at his table. He sent them into the highways and hedges to compel them to come that his house may be filled. None of those that were invited and rejected the invitation would taste of his supper.

When we reject God, it is a personal insult. Whatever reason we use, it will not stand.

Three excuses: possessions, business and natural affection. Today, people are kept from God for all kinds of reasons that make no sense. Salvation is offered. It is an engraved invitation printed in the blood of Jesus Christ. It is an invitation to the great table of salvation. Will we accept? Will we make a commitment to tell others about this great gift? Evangelism must be a part of our daily lives. We must put behind us the excuses. No more excuses. Commitment is the Word.

GOD'S IDEAL WOMAN

Who can find a virtuous woman?
For her price is far above rubies.
Proverbs 31:10-31

How many times have we read this passage? It is a favorite passage for Mother's Day, Women's Day and any day that has anything to do with women. But have we really taken a close look at this passage? Why was it written? To whom was it written?

The proverbs 31 woman is sometimes called "God's ideal woman." This does not mean that she alone represents the ideal. She is not meant to be the exact pattern for the daily activities of our lives. If she were, we - today's women - would have to grow wool and flax, spin yarn, weave fabric, dye it and then sew clothing fit for royalty.

Proverbs 31 paints a remarkable picture of the power of a woman, for good and ill. But this portrait is not simply an epilogue extolling the virtues of the ideal wife. There is more to it. Since this passage is placed at the end of proverbs, it is more likely to have been intended as a summary of what the whole book is about: depicting the person - man or woman - who is truly wise.

Just as wisdom has been depicted as a woman, so here it seems fair to see the wife as a representative figure, too. In her noble character, she stands for the kind of person we are all meant to copy. Since this passage is a model for us, let's talk about this woman of virtue whose value exceeds rubies.

Who is she?
A woman of virtue is a woman of strength. Although woman are said to be the weaker vessel, she is made strong by wisdom and grace, and the fear of God. She is not described as knowledgeable, but wise. She may not have been a learned woman as it relates to formal training, but this woman was truly wise and we know wisdom comes from God.

She is a woman who commands her own spirit. She is a woman of resolution who stands steady and firm on her principles. She is unshakable.

Who can find her?
It's not easy these days. They talk about a good man is hard to find. Well, good women are hard to find these days. There are many women who look good, have outer beauty, good parentage, wealthy, dress well, are highly educated; however, that does not mean they are virtuous.

The question we have to answer this afternoon is, what qualities must we posses as Christian women to live a life of virtue? Proverbs 31 tells us. In the 22 verses, there are at least 21 character traits. We'll look at a few.

1. **She is very industrious**. (V. 13 - 19)
She adds to the esteem of her husband. She makes him look good. She conducts herself so that he has entire confidence in her. He trusts in her chastity, her conduct, and her fidelity. When he goes away to attend to business or when he goes to work, he can trust her to keep all the affairs of home in order. As he walks out of the front door, he does not have to worry about Johnny walking in the back door.

The husband of the virtuous woman is so content with her contribution that *he shall have no need of spoil*. That means that he does not have to worry about the household money for FPL or Bell South going to the Mall for the latest Gucci bag or Ferragamo shoes or whatever the latest fashion happens to be.

The husband of this woman does not have to envy men of great wealth because he has a woman that can stretch a dime into a dollar. She is thrifty.

She shows her love to him by little niceties, sweet nothings, giving him good words and not bad ones. She doesn't tell him "you ain't no good, ain't never gonna be any good. Why you can't be like so-and-so's husband." No, No, No. She doesn't do that. She watches how she talks to him. She watches how she talks to her children. She does not yell at her children, saying things like: "Sit down stupid, with your dumb self." When you talk to anyone that way, you demean them. Virtuous women don't do that. They treat people with respect.

Her husband is known in the gates. V. 23 She adds to his reputation in the world. He leaves home smiling and looking good, shirts starched and ironed. Maybe she didn't iron them, but her servant did. As for us, if we don't iron, there is a cleaners in every neighborhood or we know an elderly lady who still has that art, like my mother.

2. She takes pains and pleasures in the duties of her household.

She hates to sit still and do nothing. Doing nothing can become a very bad habit. After so long, you'll find it hard to get up the energy or motivation to do anything. When you are tired of doing nothing, you can't stop and rest. The virtuous woman is careful to fill up time, so that none of it is lost. Time wasted can never be retrieved.

This woman rises early while it is yet night. Some high school students leave home for the bus while it is still dark, so mothers should be up early to see them off. But there are some lazy women who are still in bed when their children leave for school. Some little kids arrive at school with dirty, wrinkled clothes.

The virtuous woman does not stay up all night playing cards. She does not close the club down at night then stay in bed until time for "The Young and Restless" or what ever soap they are watching these days. She doesn't feed her children potato chips and fruit punch for dinner.

The woman of virtue takes care of her business. She doesn't try to take care of her husband's business or the business of other folk. She does whatever work is required even if it takes all the strength she has because she knows God will renew her strength.

3. She is one that makes what she does profitable.
She feels that she can make things herself better and cheaper than she can buy them. A steak grilled at home is cheaper than one from Outback or Okeechobee Steakhouse. The proverbs woman couldn't eat out. We can and we do. Times now are a little different.

After she supplies her household, she sells the excess in the market for a profit, but her home always comes first. She is a business woman as well as a wife and mother.

4. She is charitable to the poor.
She gives as much as she gets and more. She helps those who are less fortunate than herself. I saw an example of a single mother who was struggling to feed her eight children. When her sister died leaving five orphans, she took them in, not giving a second thought about how she's going to feed five extra mouths. She really didn't have a choice, so she took on that extra responsibility. I don't remember her name, but you can call her "blessed". Somehow God is going to take care of her and He's going to see that those children are fed. And who knows? He might use you or me to help feed those children.

5. She is discreet, not talkative or critical. V.26.
When she does speak, it is with wisdom and very much to the purpose. *In her tongue is the law of kindness*. The law of love and kindness is written in the heart, but it shows itself in the tongue.

Lives have been destroyed by an unflattering tongue, a tongue that spreads acid instead of honey. The tongue can be deadly. This woman that we are modeling our lives after is full of religious conversation, instead of idle gossip. As a matter fact, with all she does she still has time for her family because she does not waste a lot of time on the phone gossiping about her sisters.

8. She has the comfort and satisfaction of her virtue in her own mind (v.25).
She enjoys a firmness and constancy of mind, has spirit to bear up under many crosses and disappointments, for in this life there are pitfalls and potholes and traps waiting to trip us up. But, we've come across some bridges and conquered some obstacles. We've dealt honorably with all, *and shall rejoice in time to come;* When our footsteps get shorter and our days fewer, we will be able to look back and say "I've made my mark. I've fought a good fight. I have made many accomplishments. I was not idle or useless when I was young."

9. She is a great blessing to her relations *(v.*28)
Her children grow up and call her blessed. Her husband is so happy that he takes every chance to brag on her.

10. She gets the good word of all her neighbors.
A woman that fears the lord, shall have praise of God. She shall be highly praised (v.29): *Many have done virtuously, she excels them all.* If her children are dutiful and respectful to her, she reaps the benefit of all the care she has taken of them. Young mothers, please, give your children quality time. You will not regret it. It will pay off later on. Our own works will praise us; if our relatives and neighbors don't praise us, our good works will.

11. The *fear of the Lord* completes and crowns her character.

With all of her good qualities, this is the one thing that is most needed. The fear of God reigning in the heart is the beauty of the soul: those of who have it receive the favor of God, and in God's sight, we are valuable and precious.

You cannot put a price tag on us.

Take notice: When Proverbs 31 describes an admirable woman, her good qualities seem to be in opposition to physical beauty. Out of 22 verses, only one talks about how she looks and ladies she looks good - adorned in silk and purple, the color of wealth. Ladies you look good, too, adorned in white, the color of holiness and purity. Verse 30 says, *"Charm is deceitful, and beauty is vain, but a woman who fears the Lord, she shall be praised."*

It is the New Testament that pulls it all together by suggesting that the Godly woman gives an illusion of outward beauty. As women, we shouldn't get hung up on the features and figures we were born with. Peter tells us to "never mind the features you were born with." because *"What will adorn you with an illusion of beauty is a meek and quiet spirit, which is precious in the sight of God."* Meekness is not weakness; it is strength under control. In other words, that virtuous, beautiful woman is disciplined, chaste, discreet, deferring, gracious, controlled, "together'. This is the kind of woman that God considers Godly, which means she's got *his* qualities, and she's close to *his* heart. This is *"his'* kind of woman - his kind of beautiful, virtuous woman.

Think about how this was true in Jesus's day. The culture of his day was a Roman, pagan, woman-degrading culture. They thought little of women. They were like cattle or property. That didn't keep God from honoring the aged Anna with the sight of the new-born Messiah. It didn't keep Jesus from healing Peter's mother-in law or the woman who was hemorrhaging, or the Canaanite's woman daughter, or the woman who was bent double; It didn't keep Jesus from raising to life the synagogue official's daughter.

It didn't matter how badly society treated women, It didn't keep Jesus from honoring women.

It didn't keep Jesus from freeing the woman caught in the act of adultery, or commending the woman who poured perfume over his feet, or calling attention to the widow who gave an offering of two copper coins. It didn't keep Jesus from engaging in a long, life-saving discussion with the Samaritan woman at the well.

Oh, we are women of virtue who are precious in His sight and yes, Jesus loves us. That culture that degraded women and relegated them to second-class status didn't keep Jesus from having some of God's beautiful women as some of his very best friends: Mary and Martha, Mary Magdalene, Joanne, Susanna, and others. Beautiful women were the closest to the cross when he died, and the first to see him when he came back to life.

I can bring it closer to today. It wasn't until 1920 that women in this country were given the right to vote. And that didn't include us. It was years later when African Americans were given the right to vote. But it didn't stop

Jesus from loving us.

There is a place for us, ladies, in this world. We are blessed that our culture is not as it was when Jesus walked the earth. We have great opportunities. We are free to use the greatness that He placed in us; but we must be ever so careful to use it for His glory.

We must be determined not to abuse this strength we have. It is not a physical strength. It is a moral force; an intellectual force; it is power by reason of influence and it's a source of encouragement. That's the kind of strength we have.

God's longest description of his ideal woman ends with these words: *"These good deeds of hers shall bring her honor and recognition from even the leaders of the nations."*

This woman of virtue runs her household with her hand, her head, and her heart. Looking around in the sanctuary and in our neighborhoods, we see you. You are women who are leaders in your chosen field- You are educators and entrepreneurs; engineers and lawyers; mortgage brokers and bankers. You are graphic artists and computer programmers; You are in housekeeping and hotel management; healthcare and real estate; and ministry and marketing. You are successful at anything you put your hands to.

Some people spend a lot of time trying to figure out what we should be allowed to do, but God says in his word, a woman can do anything. It's not what we do, it's who we are and whose we are. When we are wise and full of kind words, when we are hard-working and conscientious and deeply reverent in our love for God - in other words, if we are virtuous women with a meek and quiet spirit - we can do anything in the whole wide world, and the world will praise us for it.

We are women of virtue, handmade by God to fulfill wonderful plans of his. We need to be sure, very sure that we know what His plan is for us. If we line up in His will and stay in His Word, everything will be all right. Christian women of virtue, you are God's ideal woman.

May God bless you and keep you.

THE HIGH ROAD TO SUCCESS

FINALLY!!! Graduation day. You have waited a long time for this moment. I understand your excitement. The first leg of the journey is over, but tonight, the second leg begins. The Highway to Success lies before you. Are you ready for the trip of a lifetime?

I know you are ready to celebrate, so I will speak to you very briefly tonight about the high road to success. Believe it or not there is a low road; but that road takes short cuts and only leads to a temporary success, while the high road leads to lasting success.

Random House Webster's college Dictionary defines success as the attainment of wealth, position, honors, or the like. I believe a better definition is achieving goals you set for yourself. If a goal has been set and met, that's success.

There are some basic common truths you must remember in order to be successful.

1. Be your best. That shows noble character. Success won at the cost of self respect is not success.

2. Do your best. That's the quality of your performance. The difference between failure and success is performing a task nearly right and doing it exactly right.

3. Work hard. That's the quantity of your performance. You see, there are no secrets to success. It is the result of preparation, hard work and learning from failure.

4. **Never, never, never, never give up**. That's persistence.

On this journey to a place called success, there are no nonstop flights. There are stops and detours, departures and arrivals.

Depart from **Mediocrity** and arrive at **Excellence**.
Depart from **Procrastination** and arrive at **Action.**
Depart from **Incompetence** and arrive at **Brilliance.**
Depart from **Nonchalance** and arrive at **Commitment.**
Depart from "**I Can't**" and arrive at "**I Can**."

I Have an example of that last departure from "I can't" . Some years ago, one of my daughters was preparing for the "Miss Florida Drill Team" competition. The contestants were traditionally seniors in high school, but she was only a junior.

After having difficulty choreographing her routine, she became frustrated. I could see what was coming and I was prepared. When she said to me, " I can't do this," I told her to get the dictionary, look up the word 'can't' and read it to me. She flipped the pages. When she turned to the page where the word "can't" should have been, it was not there. You see, I had already cut the word out with a razor blade. I don't know what was on the other side of "can't" but whatever it was that word was gone, too. My point was, if the word is not in *our* dictionary, never mind other folk's dictionaries, it's not a real word, so don't use it anymore. She didn't - and she went on to win the title convincingly.

So, graduates, take that word, 'can't' out of your vocabulary and your journey to success on the high road will be a little easier.

You know as well as I do, there are very few (if any) "overnight successes" You didn't get here overnight. Did you? You had night after night after night successes.... And on most of those nights you were burning the midnight oil; learning medical terms and procedures, preparing for exams. It was not always easy.

Sometimes it required an **extra** measure of motivation . You had to have the motivation to work hard, when "*taking it easy*" was always a temptation.

It's good to know that success isn't by the position you reach in life; it's measured by the obstacles you overcome. And when you're taking the high road to success, there are pitfalls, potholes that you have to step over.

The mere fact that you are here tonight, shows that you have what it takes to travel the high road. I can relate to your efforts. I know what you've been through. I've sat where you are sitting. Some of you have a gap in the time you finished high school and the time you enrolled at Medical Career Institute. I was 30 years old with a family, a job and responsibilities when I decided I could do better by going back to school. There were times when I almost gave up. But I didn't and you didn't and that's why we are all here tonight.

Now that you have finished your course, please remember what drew you to seek a medical career. As you work in your chosen field, enjoy your work, develop good working relationships and be open to new opportunities.

Don't even open the door to discouragement. If you are not finding the acceptance and success you desire today, just remember, your success story is still being written. And if by chance you fail at a task, don't panic. Failure is a teacher - a harsh one, but the best. You learn from your mistake.

Allow me to share this story. The late, great Ray Charles was able to do what few musicians could - create music that appealed to young and old, black and white, rich and poor. He successfully crossed major boundaries. Ray Charles lost both of his parents and a brother before he was grown. He grew up in a school for the blind where he learned to play piano and sing. By the time he was a teenager, he was a hit in Central and North Florida. He and his friends believed in his talent.
In 1946, Lucky Millender, the famed band leader, brought his band to Orlando. Ray Charles managed to get an

audition. What an opportunity. It was his first chance at the big time.

Charles sang and played with all his might. He gave 150 percent. Millender listened quietly. At the end of the audition Charles expected to hear praise, but all he heard was silence and finally Millender told Ray, *"Kid, you ain't good enough."* Ray could not believe his ears. He had performed with all his heart, with every fiber of his being. He couldn't have heard right. So he asked Millender to repeat what he said. Lucky Millender said, *"You heard right. You don't got what it takes."*

Ray went back to his room, heartbroken. He cried for days. But when he had no more tears to shed, something happened on the inside. He knew he was not a quitter. He knew he had God-given talent; so he began to practice as never before. Looking back years later, Charles realized that failure was the best thing that ever happened to him. He vowed that no one would ever be able to say that about him again. And we know the rest of the story.

Graduates, success consists of getting up more times than you fall. **Never** accept another person's assessment of your talent and skill. **Never** let someone tell you what you cannot do. **Never** take shortcuts that impugn your integrity. **Never** step down from the high road.
I conclude with the familiar poem by Edgar Guest.

> Somebody said that it couldn't be done,
> But he with a chuckle replied
> That "maybe it couldn't," but he would be one
> Who wouldn't say so till he tried.
>
> So he buckled right in with the trace of a grin
> On his face. If he worried he hid it.

He started to sing as he tackled the thing
That couldn't be done and he did it.

Somebody scoffed, "Oh, you'll never do that;
At least no one has ever done it"
But he took of his coat and he took off his hat, and the first thing
we knew He'd begun it.
With a lift of his chin and a bit of a grin,
without any doubt or quiddit.
He started to sing as he tackled the thing
That couldn't be done and he did it.

Graduates, there are thousands to tell you it cannot be done,
There are thousands to prophesy failure;
There are thousands to point out to you, one by one,
The dangers that wait to assail you,
But just buckle in with a bit of a grin.
Just take off your coat and go to it;
Just start to sing as you tackle the thing
That "cannot be done" and you'll do it.

Medical Career Institute graduates of 2008, your accomplishment is major. I salute you. Congratulations and may God bless you.

RETIREMENT BANQUET

We are here tonight to celebrate many years of a blessed ministry. Miracle Revival Deliverance Center has been a birthing room for new ministries. Some of the babies are here tonight. Who can count the ministries that were born out of this ministry?

Many ministries represented here tonight came thru the birthing room at Miracle Revival. From the home of Reverend and Mother Johnson to a store-front church on Spruce Avenue to the church on the corner of 33rd and Old Dixie to the present location at 37th Street and Old Dixie Highway - all along the way, people have come and gone.

Miracle Revival has been a temporary home, a training ground. Seeds that were planted there, germinated and grew elsewhere. In this room tonight are seeds, saplings and strong Oak trees. God is a God of seed. When Abraham could not produce a seed, God gave him a seed. Abraham became the Father of Faith and the father of many nations. When we ask for Oak trees, He answers with acorns. We need to be perceptive enough to know that the Oak tree we asked for is in the acorn.

There came a time in the ministry at Miracle Revival to say goodbye. Sometimes, as children, we do not want to leave the comfortable nest. But when God says, it's time to grow up, time to start your own ministry, you have to move. Some of you gladly answered the call and you left. But for some of you, God had to trouble the waters in order to push you out. All mothers know that no baby is born without some pushing. Some of the ministries wouldn't be here tonight if there had not been a whole lot of pushing going on.

Pushing is an essential part of the birthing process. To illustrate this, there is a story about the emperor butterfly. The emperor butterfly, after it has gone through its various development stages, begins to break out of its cocoon. As it pushes through, the insect strains because the hole in the cocoon is smaller than the butterfly. But it pushes and pushes.....and it is painful....and it is a struggle.

One time, a little boy was looking as this natural process of pushing and the struggling, and the painful efforts of this butterfly trying to get out of the cocoon. In a darkroom, the boy watched this beautiful butterfly pushing, straining, wiggling, trying to exit the cocoon until he could see the insect's pulsating body. After watching this for a while, the boy decided he would help. Carefully he picked up the cocoon, took out his knife and just slit the hole a little in the cocoon so that the butterfly would not have to struggle so much. Well, after receiving help from human hands, the butterfly did not have to struggle nearly as much. But something interesting happened. When the butterfly got out of the cocoon, it was beautiful, but it couldn't fly. You see, the pushing and straining and pain sends blood into the butterfly's veins to develop its wings so that when the butterfly comes out of the cocoon, it is able to fly. Never interrupt God's natural process.

There are times when God sees us pushing, straining, struggling, and trying to get out. And what Reverend Johnson and Mother Johnson understand is what we all need to understand and that is: Cutting a hole would make things easier, but we will not fly! Sometimes God has to let us push, strain, and struggle so when we come out, we can celebrate the pushing, straining, and struggling. While we are pushing, straining and struggling, we must remember that God sees us while we are pushing. God is watching us struggle, and is there to protect us if anything were to happen.

The bountiful fruit of much labor is here tonight and we are grateful to God for that. We serve a good God. He is a God of seed and a God of promise.

Sometimes, we find ourselves wondering, God, what is your plan for my life? Where am I going to be in five years? Ten Years? What will I be doing? Thirty-nine years ago, I worshiped with the small band of believers at the store-front on Spruce Avenue. While I was only there for a year, I never forgot my experiences. Since that time my life has taken many detours. But every twist and every turn led me closer to spiritual maturity. Sometimes, we get discouraged when we suffer setbacks, but God's chosen people had a forty-year setback in the wilderness and they still survived. We will too. Some people say He is the God of a second chance. I say He is the God of another chance and another chance and another chance.

Miracle Revival is still on the front line of the battle. It's not over yet. We are all in a war. We all have a great job to do today. We all are kingdom soldiers. We have to forget our differences and unite in this war against evil. Our nation is in trouble. Our nation needs a healing.

Why do we need a healing in this country? Look around you. Listen to the news. Read the paper. Check out what's going on in your own household.

On Wednesday of this week, Judge Alfred Goodwin, a senior member of the 9th Circuit Court of Appeals in California, wrote an opinion that having public school children recite the pledge is unconstitutional because of the phrase -"one nation under God." This affects nine western states. And while that decision is now on hold, how much longer before it will affect these entire United States.

We, the body of believers have stood back and allowed things like this to happen. Instead of fighting against this, we have fought against each other. We stayed back and let one atheist, Madelyn Murray O'Hara, singlehandedly take prayer out of the school. But I ask you tonight, who took prayer out of the home?

How long will we linger in complacency while the enemy works his schemes? How long will we allow one atheist after another to run rough-shod over us? How long will we dwell on petty differences instead of uniting to fight these battles? How long will we allow the devil to put blinders on our eyes while the real war is being waged around us? How long, body of Christ, how long?

Paul told us in Romans that we are more than conquerors. We don't act like it. We go to church on Sundays and we dance and shout and we come home and say, "Didn't we have church today?" But what are we doing Monday thru Friday?

If we could just rise above this physical world and look down through the eyes of God, we would see a valley of dry bones. That's what we look like.

There's an ankle bone over there in the Methodist church and a leg bone over there in the Pentecostal church. Around the corner, there's a hip bone in the Catholic church. Up the street, there's a leg bone in the Baptist church; down the street, there's a knee bone in the Episcopalian church. Bones are scattered all over the place. *"Son of man, can these bones live?"* We have to rise up, connect and become a whole body if we are going to fight this war.

We're not effective, because we are splintered. We have children not speaking to parents, brothers and sisters who don't talk to each other - disjointed families. God is not pleased.

Our children are faltering in school and flunking the course called "LIFE." We have children on crack cocaine, our sons and grandsons are in jail; our babies are having babies and tired grandmothers who are raising their second and third set of children are crying out to God, saying, "Lord, when do I get a break?"

We have children failing the FCAT in great numbers, endangering their chances of one day getting a high school diploma. I don't mean a piece of paper that says you attended school for twelve years, but one that says you are qualified to get a decent job or attend somebody's college. We pass small children playing in the street on Sundays as we make our way to church. Some of them have never set foot in a church. What are we doing about this, body of Christ? We are praising and worshiping on Sundays, but when are we serving? What are we doing the rest of the week?

Saints. Its time to close ranks against the enemy. It's time to circle the wagons and do battle in the real war. This war is not carnal, it is spiritual. Our nation is under attack. Why? Because this country is rapidly spreading the gospel to every corner of the world. Look at TBN and the powerful satellites that proclaim the gospel to remote countries. The enemy knows that once everyone has heard the gospel, Christ's return is imminent. The enemy has no choice but to wage a full battle against the United States.

Only God can help us with this battle. He has made us some promises: II Chronicles 7:14 lets us know that He is a God of promise. But it also gives us prerequisites for those promises. *"If my people which are called by My name, shall humble themselves, and pray, and seek My face, and turn from their wicked ways; then will hear from heaven, and will forgive their sin; and will heal their land."*

In view of the tragedy that happened in our nation on Sept 11, 2001, this scripture is very important. We need to take a look at it.

There are four things we need to do to benefit form God's promise to heal our land. Be humble, pray, seek God and turn from our wicked ways. Just four things. Of the four things God could have listed first, he listed "humble." How do we humble ourselves? The first step is confession, but how do we know what to confess. We need to ask Him. David has given us an excellent example - The searchlight prayer. *"Search me, O God, and know my heart; try me, and know my thoughts: And see if there be any wicked way in me, and lead me in the way everlasting"* Psalm 139:23,24

We need God to turn the light on us. We need God to look deep inside and see if our heart has been circumcised. "Search me God. God, if I've done anything, please Lord, reveal it to me so I may confess." This searchlight prayer is truly a part of the humbling process. The psalmist tells us *"if we regard iniquity in our hearts,"* God will not hear us.

After God shows us our real heart, we agree with Him, ask for mercy. I John 1:9 says *"If we confess our sins, he is faithful and just to forgive our sins, to cleanse us from righteousness."*

After we humble ourselves, we are ready to bring our

petitions to God. At this point, we have already prayed and asked God to search our hearts, and agreed with the things He has revealed to us. Now what would we ask for? Petitions are "asking prayers." We should ask God for things consistent with the promises of God. Let us not fail to ask God to continue blessing Reverend Johnson, Mother Johnson and the birthing room at Miracle Revival.

When we get to know God better, some of these other things that we're asking will begin to diminish in importance. This is when we start becoming a partner with God in prayer. The majority of our petitions to God should be *"Lord, change me. Lord, let your kingdom come into my life. Lord, help me to be a better servant."* For a few minutes, we should forget about husbands, cars, children, health, careers. Let's learn to seek Him first and He'll add all of these other things to us.

Now we have humbled ourselves, we have prayed. Now it's time to seek God's face. And the first step in seeking is the prayer of unconditional surrender. In this prayer, we tell God that nothing matters to us more than His Spirit controlling us. This may well be the most important prayer we pray. If we do not pray this prayer, most other praying will be in vain.

As African Americans, we have looked to the government, family members, our jobs and other things to be the provider of our needs, but God is our Jehovah-Jireh, our provider. We have looked to many things. We looked to guns for our protection. We looked to preachers and evangelists to teach and guide us. We have sought strength in organizations, church structures and legislation. We have looked for our worth and acceptance in positions and titles. We need to repent of having all of these gods before the one and only true God. He is our all and we have to look to Him for everything.

Our circumstances may be battling us down to the ground. But we need to know what kind of God we serve. And if we read His word, diligently, there will be no doubt. Just think about the fact that we have the right to go to God in prayer. We can go into the throne room to have a private audience with the One who holds the world in His hand. That's awesome. Meditate on that.

And finally, when we have humbled ourselves, prayed, searched for God, now it's time to turn...and when we turn, we go in a different direction.

We choose the New Instead of the Old. We turn to victorious living. We change our ways of thinking and responding. We no longer respond in the flesh because that blocks the Holy Spirit from changing our soul.

It's up to us to look to the Word of God and make the decision to change. Naturally, we can refuse to turn and experience more of the enemy's slings and arrows in our lives and the lives of our families. The process is painful. It means letting go of habits and attitudes and relationships with which we have grown accustomed. When we decide to make that change - we have to press our way. No looking back across our shoulders. There is nothing back there for us. Everything is in front of us. Yes, the process is painful, but we have to go the distance.

America has been and is still guilty. There needs to be corporate confession in this country. Because if we don't humble ourselves as a nation and pray and seek God's face and turn from our wicked ways, God is going to deal with us and He will use our enemies to chastise us.

Humbling ourselves, praying, seeking God, and turning from our wicked ways are all elements in the healing process. These are things we must do in order to benefit from the blessing and promises of God.

I close this message by saying to every person, every ministry here:

Out of your bellies shall flow rivers - not drops, not dribbles, but rivers of living water. You have power you haven't even used yet. You have strength you have not accessed yet. You have glory you haven't discovered yet. Your best days you haven't seen yet.

God has placed something special in each of you. It's in you to be great. It's in you to overcome. It's in you to be victorious. It's in you to live and not die. It's in you to be the head and not the tail. It's in you to prosper and succeed. It's in you to make it. It's in you to go forward. What God has for you, it is for you and no one can take it away.

And to Reverend and Mother Johnson, stay prayerful, stay focused, continue pushing, and know this: For every tear you had to shed, for every pain you felt, for every broken heart, God has blessings that you can't even begin to comprehend. So be encouraged. For every ministry you birthed, there is a star in your crown. May God continue blessing each of you abundantly.

27TH Annual Reomia Bennett Stevens Scholarship Luncheon

Leadership and Service

"If you would be king of all, you must become the servant of all." Zig Zeiglar, the great motivator, said, "You can best achieve what you want in life if you are servant enough to help others achieve what they want in life." I will be speaking today from your theme: Leadership and service.

My emphasis is *Servant-hood Leadership*. One who leads, also serves. Leadership and service are indispensable to each other. Sometimes, people start out as leaders and end up becoming bosses.

There is a difference in leadership and boss-hood. H. Gordon Selfridge gave the following differences:

> The boss drives his men; the leader coaches them.
> The boss depends on authority; the leader on goodwill.
> The boss inspires fear; the leader inspires enthusiasm.
> The boss says, "I"; the leader says "we."
> The boss knows how its done; the leader shows how it's done.
> The boss says "go"; the leader says "let's go."

There are four keys to Servant-hood Leadership.

I. VISION
Where there is no vision, the people perish. If a group, whether business, church or government, is under a leader with no vision, the result is, disorder, rebellion, chaos, and at worst - anarchy. There have been some visionary leaders down through history. Mary McLeod Bethune had a vision that she could educate young black men and women. Harriet Tubman had a vision that she could lead people to freedom.

In 1942, eleven women at the Lewis Business School in Detroit Michigan had a vision that they could create a place where women of color could connect, express and share; thus we have Eta Phi Beta Sorority that promotes and develops closer fellowship among business and professional women.

Vision Axioms

1. Nothing happens to us by accident; all reversals are God-given challenges.

2. Never sidestep challenges. A challenge is like a charging bull. Grab that bull by the horns and slap him twice across the face and let him know that God is in charge of you, and you're in charge of him.

3. Love people, use things Never, ever reverse this order. If you do you will become inhuman and unworthy of the high character of God's servants.

4. Don't celebrate leisure and condemn hard work. Put leisure and labor side by side, and value them both. Leisure will give your life pacing. Labor will make you productive.

If you can remember these four beliefs, you will find your vision survives all challenges. And you will be challenged. Do you not know that Mary McLeod Bethune was challenged when she started talking about building a school? Don't you know that people told her, "You must be crazy!"

She only had a dollar fifty in her pocket, but she had a dream like steel in her soul. She was unshakeable. We need to understand the inherent power of vision, where that power comes from and how to hold on to it. We must be able to match our personal dreams and visions to those of the organization.

Your national president, Louise Hoskins Broadnax will only be effective if she can rally all of her sorors in every chapter to the dream that she has to move this organization forward.

II. DECISION
In a poem entitled "The Road Not Taken" Robert Frost said, "Two roads diverged in a wood, and I- I took the one less traveled by, and that has made all the difference." Sometimes, it's a decision that makes all the difference in the world.

Leaders are decision makers; they are decisive , not waverers. Sometimes we make decisions that are not always right. Sometimes it's a matter of timing.

The wrong decision at the wrong time = DISASTER.
The wrong decision at the right time = MISTAKE.

The right decision at the wrong time = REJECTION.
The right decision at the right time = SUCCESS.

An American umpire said "It ain't nothin' til I call it."

A vision is nothing until we *decide* to do something about it. A decision must be made. If the eleven women at Lewis Business School had not decided to turn their vision into reality, this scholarship luncheon would not be taking place.

III. NETWORKING
The leader of a large Christian organization, R. C. Sproul, said, "I *hope when I die there will be at least five of my friends who will be able to sit through my funeral without looking at their watches*." Our friends make up our network.

Your chapter president, Hyacinthia Becton, is not a lone ranger. I can believe that Louise Hoskins Broadnax, your national president, is not a lone ranger, either. As a matter of fact she stated that "networking is one of the greatest strengths of Eta Phi Beta Sorority." Leadership does not exist in a vacuum. A great leader knows that great leadership is teamwork. Those who follow must also lead from time to time. A person who cannot follow will not make a great leader.

This team comprises the network. Behind every great leader is a great network of a great many friends. This Scholarship luncheon did not come about from the efforts of one woman. Someone had to secure this site. Someone was in charge of publicity. Someone had to work on the Souvenir Program. Someone had to get the speaker and *everybody* had to sell tickets. It was teamwork.

A good example of networking is Jesus Christ. Whether you are Jewish, Christian, or Moslem, you have to acknowledge that He is the best example of servanthood leadership. He trained a network of twelve men who carried on the work when He was gone. They in turn, trained others. The impact of that networking is felt today. One leader and twelve followers turned the world upside down. *Networking multiplies our power.*

IV. ACTION
To bring a vision into reality, a decision must be made, a network formed and action taken. It boils down to just three little words: **Just do it.**

All of us who serve and lead, make an impact on the world around us.

Allow me to introduce a woman who embodies servant-hood leadership.

Bertha Knox Gilkey
They called the tenement housing where Bertha's mother used to live the "quadroon." It had a dirt floor, no hot and cold running water and the windows were made out of something like wax paper. Everyone in the quadroon had outside toilets.

When they moved to Cochran, it was like moving to heaven. They finally had hot and cold running water. When Cochran was all white, they didn't refer to it as a project; it was called Cochran Gardens. But when it became more and more black, services were reduced and Cochran became a dumping ground.

Bertha's mother had fifteen children living in a three bedroom apartment. There was no recreation, nothing to do, no jobs, no nothing. Bertha watched women - black women and poor white women - struggle to make a community, a neighborhood, with nothing. Then she watched millions of dollars come from the anti-poverty programs.

In 1974, the city of St. Louis voted to tear Cochran down. Bertha said, "Over my dead body. We 've been here through

all the bad times and we're gonna be here for the good times."
But Bertha had to beg people to stay, especially in the winter
when the lights were out, the heater wouldn't heat and the
pipes burst all over. Bertha had a plan.

She took the gang leaders, second and third offenders, and
created renovation crews. The same kids that were normally
vandalizing and setting units on fire, were now restoring them.
Bertha started at fourteen years old being concerned about
other people. She became an activist for welfare and tenant
rights. She didn't stop until tenants were given the right to
manage their property. Today they control their own destiny,
they control how they live, how their children live, all because
Bertha was a woman who believed in service to others.

She was a leader who had a *vision* that people could control
their own destiny, that they did not have to live in a dumping
ground. She made a *decision* to act on that vision. And she
built her *network* with gang leaders and troublemakers to turn
a project around. She took *action*. She is a fine example of
servanthood leadership, not for herself, but for others.

When we are leaders, we make an impact on the world around
us. It can be positive or negative, direct or indirect depending
on what kind of leader we are. Hitler was a leader, but look at
the impact he had versus the impact of Mahatma Gandhi or
Martin Luther King, Jr.

Ladies, of Eta Phi Beta Sorority, it does not yet appear what
kind of impact you have had and will have. If every student
that this sorority has helped nationwide over its 63 year history
could be tracked, you would be amazed at the impact you have
made in this country. Who can gage the extent of your
influence? Who knows the magnitude of what your efforts
over the years have accomplished?   We never know where
life's roads will lead us and what the end will be. Who knew
that the little baby girl born in a row house on the edge of a

bean field in a migrant field would be standing before you today as your speaker?

To the students and scholarship recipients in the audience today, I say congratulations . Don't let your education nor the lack thereof, nor the status of your birth or your economic status limit you. As you embark on another level of your education, we send you off with our love, our prayers and a new alphabet.

Graduates, this is for you.

A is for your **attitude** and that determines your altitude - how high you fly in this life.
B is for **best.** Anything less is not an option.
C is for **courage**. Be bold in what you stand for, but careful in what you fall for.
D is for **determination** to go forth with confidence.
E is for **effort** you must make to be superb.
F is for **faith** and that is belief without proof.
G is for the **greatness** that God has placed in each of you.
H is for **honor** for your ancestors, your country, your God, and yourself.
I is for **imagination** which strengthens desire and fosters action.
J is for **justice** - fight for it.
K is for **kindness,** a language that the deaf can hear and the blind can see.
L is for **love** - that's what makes the world go 'round.
M is for **morality** - be above board in all your actions.
N is for **never** - never give up.
O is for **opportunity** to put your education to good use.
P is for **prayer** - pray about everything, worry about nothing.
Q is for **quest** - seek knowledge.
R is for **reflections** - take time to look inward.
S is for **strength** to stand when others are falling.
T is for **test**- life will test you again and again.

U is for **unity** that we as a people must achieve.

V is for **valor** in facing danger.

W is for **winners** and winners never quit.

X is for **x-ray** - learn to look beneath the surface.

Y is for **you** and your contribution.

Z is for the **zeal** you must have for the gospel of Jesus Christ.

May God bless and keep each of you.

www.ingramcontent.com/pod-product-compliance
Lightning Source LLC
LaVergne TN
LVHW051521080426
835509LV00017B/2144